THE BOY
AND HIS
SAND CASTLE

A Journey of Redemption

By Zakaria Amara

Artist and Designer:
Agata Filipczak
(Niokoba)

The chapter titled "Nightmares and Daydreams" was previously
published by Scalawag magazine.

Cover Design, Typesetting, and Interior Design: Agata Filipczak (Niokoba, www.niokoba.com)

Library and Archives Canada Cataloguing in Publication

The Boy and His Sandcastle: A Journey of Redemption

ISBN: 978-1-7382393-0-6 (paperback)
ISBN: 978-1-7382393-2-0 (hardcover)
ISBN: 978-1-7382393-1-3 (ebook)

A cataloging record for this publication is available
from the Library and Archives Canada.

Editing:
Sana Abuleil
Valerie Jones

Calligraphy:
Omar Uddin

To my sister,
for saving my life.

CONTENTS

INTRODUCTION

By Dena Amara

It's a Saturday afternoon, and the atmosphere feels similar to the Wild West. Having just polished off our pasta lunch, we're brimming with energy. As I glance over, I spot Zak climbing the doorway, momentarily distracting me from the remnants of pasta sauce adorning my face. Excitement bubbles within me as I cheer him on, urging him to reach the top. When he finally conquers the climb, I can't help but jump up and down as Mama captures the moment with her camera.

Reflecting on my childhood in Saudi Arabia, I'm flooded with fond memories, largely thanks to Zak's knack for orchestrating moments of joy. In a place where outdoor fun was a rarity, especially for girls, Zak and I were like characters from a classic cartoon, constantly engaged in a playful back-and-forth. Despite being two years younger than him, we sparred, played, laughed, and repeated the cycle endlessly. Zak's desire to push beyond boundaries often landed him in trouble, but I was always there, acting as his steadfast protector whenever the need arose. As the years passed, our bond deepened, even when it seemed like we were navigating different paths. Through it all, I held onto the unwavering belief that family transcends all else.

Then, on June 2, 2006, my world shattered. Everything suddenly felt incomprehensible. I was over 10,000 kilometers away when news of his arrest reached me, and it took weeks to return to Canada. While reading about the events was one thing; seeing my brother clad in an orange jumpsuit behind a pane of glass was an entirely different ordeal to process. How does one make sense of such a human experience? How do I continue living a semblance of a normal life while my brother languishes behind bars? How do I maintain my role as his 'Protector'? Nothing in my life had prepared me for this. Despite the confusion, one thing was certain: I had made a vow to myself never to abandon him, regardless of the cost. Little did I realize the depth of that commitment, the sacrifices it would entail, and how long it would endure.

During Zak's time at Maplehurst prison, "The Don Jail," and the Special Handling Unit, connecting with him on an emotional and intellectual level proved immensely challenging. During our visits, I'd peer into his eyes, searching for the brother who once filled my childhood with fun and adventure. But he seemed elusive, lost within himself. Despite this, I clung to the belief that he was still there, somewhere deep within. Refusing to accept the idea of losing him, I devised a plan to remain a constant presence in his life, visiting him regularly and ensuring I never missed a call. Though he appeared to be giving up on himself, I refused to do the same. With unwavering support, I hoped he would sense my love and find his way back to himself.

In the ninth year of Zak's incarceration, he was finally granted a transfer to Millhaven Maximum Security prison in Kingston, Ontario. Accompanied by our elder brother, I scheduled a visit and made our way there. This marked the first time I was able to see my brother without a glass barrier and embrace him. Our reunion was surreal. Zak held my hands the entire time as if to make sure he was not dreaming.

Not long after his transfer, Zak's progress began to accelerate. I witnessed a transformation—a man once prone to fleeing from his problems now stood firm in facing them head-on. I watched as Zak confronted his past, delving into every painful memory, seeking solace within the pages of books, and gradually steering his life in a new direction, one step at a time. From a confused, emotionally-distant individual, he transformed into a mature, self-aware, growth-oriented person.

Zak also began to actively participate in events organized at Millhaven, and joined both the poetry club and book club, which were run by Michael Hurley and Gordon Darrall (who continue to be in his life to this day). It was also during this time that he met someone I consider a hero, Sena Hussain. Sena was the editor of *Cell Count*, a publication which circulated throughout Canada and featured writings and artwork from inmates. With Sena's encouragement and support, Zak delved into the world of creative writing. They say that voicing something aloud compels you to confront it. This proved true for Zak. As he began to pen his thoughts, he confronted his past in ways that offered only two options: remain trapped or embrace healing and self-liberation.

In 2019, Zak was transferred to Warkworth Medium Security prison in Brighton, Ontario. Until then, I had resigned myself to the belief that my brother's incarceration was a life sentence with no room for hope. However, encounters with individuals who challenged this notion gradually altered my mindset. Despite lacking concrete evidence, I realized there was no reason Zak shouldn't pursue parole. And so, with the support of many and a considerable amount of courage, we pushed for Zak's release in 2021. However, despite our best efforts, the outcome was disheartening – a rejection that felt like a significant setback, plunging us deeper into despair.

The setback affected both Zak and me profoundly. Nevertheless, we were left with only two choices: to succumb to hopelessness or to persevere and continue our journey of healing and growth. I understood that bravery and resilience were essential to successfully pursue the latter course. Together, I reassured Zak that we would overcome our circumstances and forge a path towards brighter days.

Despite facing numerous obstacles, our determination remained unwavering, and in October 2022, Zak was finally granted parole, marking a new chapter in our journey towards freedom and redemption. On November 9, 2022, I set off for Warkworth, filled with anticipation and dreams I'd held onto for seventeen long years. Somewhere along the way, amidst the challenges and setbacks, I had resigned myself to accepting life as it was. Yet here I was on my way to pick up my long-lost brother. Arriving at Warkworth, I parked my car as instructed and waited with bated breath, stealing glances at the rear-view mirror until, *finally*, there he was. With a surge of emotion, I leaped out of the car, eager to assist him with his belongings. As our eyes met, we shared a knowing smile, acknowledging the magnitude of what we had achieved together. It was a moment of triumph, one that seemed almost surreal as we drove away, still trying to grasp the reality of it all.

As I drove my brother home that day, tears of joy streamed down my face. For the first time in almost two decades, I felt whole again. The void that had consumed me was finally filled. After countless restless nights spent worrying, my prayers had been answered.

I glanced over at Zak sitting beside me, his eyes twinkling with renewed hope. At that moment, I knew our journey was far from over. Together, we would continue healing, rediscovering the beautiful world and all its possibilities. I made a silent promise to appreciate every single moment, no matter how small. This redemption story was never just about my brother. It is a testament to the human capacity for change, forgiveness, and love. If we open our hearts, there are second chances. The road to redemption has its twists and turns, but the destination makes the arduous journey worthwhile. And worth sharing.

As I pulled into the driveway of his halfway house, memories of childhood laughter echoed in my mind. With Zak finally home, I had reclaimed a piece of us that was lost. Our family was made whole once more. This profoundly moving, lifelong quest has taught me that true freedom comes from within. As long as we cling to hope and stand united, sustained by love and compassion, the light can never be extinguished.

08.00 بسم الله الرحمن الرحيم *A*

"In the name of God, the Most Compassionate, the Most Merciful."*

*The beginning of a diary entry from 1996, written when I was eleven-years-old.

The words you are about to read were born in the crucible of confinement, under the haunting shadow of an indefinite prison sentence. Midwifed by inspiration rather than premeditation, they chronicle my journey as I struggled to come to terms with an unyielding and intolerable reality.

In many ways, this work is a testament to the power of the written word —where the pen proves mightier than the sword. Sailing on a surging sea of ink, these prison walls could not confine me. And now, I am finally here with you.

This is your story, as well…

DESOLATION

The Boy and his Sandcastle

Spring, 2018

My beloved twelve-year-old daughter asked me to share my story with you. I am having a hard time with where to start, what to write, and how much to unveil. Perhaps I should begin from the present and make my way back to the past.

I've been in prison for twelve years now. In 2010, I received a life sentence after pleading guilty to being one of the ringleaders of the "Toronto 18" terror plot. Thankfully, no one was physically hurt. I was 20-years-old then, and I am almost 33 now.

In pre-trial custody, I was deemed a radical threat to the inmate population, and so, I was involuntarily placed in solitary confinement for three years. After receiving my sentence, I was once again considered a radical threat and sent to the Special Handling Unit, Canada's only super-max prison. (Usually, you would have to kill or stab someone inside to be eligible for such a transfer.) After spending six horrifying years there, I was finally transferred to Millhaven Max, where I currently reside.

Given this information, it wouldn't be a huge leap to assume I'm a tough, violent, and angry man with a threatening demeanour. But truthfully, I am the exact opposite.

Guilty, I am.
Radicalized, I was.

Yet, I still find my entire situation incredibly surreal. I often go back in time to retrace my steps in search of clues—anything—that can tell me how I ended up here. But every time I engage in this exercise, I stumble across a young man who was caught up in a perfect storm of internal and external influences. The inevitability of it all is what I find most remarkable.

After any major terrorist attack, there is usually a fierce debate about what makes individuals susceptible to radical ideologies. Unfortunately, this rarely occurs when the perpetrators are non-Muslims (Right-wing extremists in the U.S., for example). But if I had a noose around my neck, and the only thing that could save my life was the answer to this dumbfounding question, then I would have to say that it is the emotional state of feeling utterly humiliated and worthless.

I have always felt worthless. I still struggle with this feeling to this day. Perhaps I feel this way because I carry within me a strong inner critic that has been ripping me apart since I was a child. Or maybe it's because I have always felt like an outsider. You see, even though I am a citizen of this country, I have never felt Canadian. For whatever reason, ever since I arrived here as a twelve-year-old boy, in my mind, to be a real Canadian, you had to be white.

Before immigrating to Canada, I lived in my mother's country of birth, Cyprus. There, too, I felt like an outsider, since I was keenly aware that my Arab features automatically disqualified me from claiming to be Cypriot.

Before that, I lived in Saudi Arabia, where native citizens are infamous for looking down upon all non-Saudis. I still remember the words of a Saudi boy who referred to me as "Phalas-Teezi" (a hybrid word that combines "Palestinian" with the Arabic word for "ass"). The sad fact that I was sexually molested while living there could have only intensified my inner feelings of worthlessness and inadequacy.

Even in Jordan, my own country of birth, I never considered myself Jordanian, since I belonged to a family that originally came to Jordan as refugees after losing their land to the Israeli occupation.

Many of you have probably wondered why the Muslim world has produced so many radicalized individuals in the recent past. Blaming Islam for it is incredibly simplistic, if not absolutely wrong. When I look at what the people of that region have gone through over the last century, I am surprised that there aren't more extremists, not less. I can't imagine how utterly worthless many of them have been made to feel. The culprits are foreign and local governments who systematically strip powerless human beings of their dignity.

What happens to a street vendor who can't sell his fruits without having to pay a bribe to a policeman?

What happens to a young man or woman who just graduated from university, but can't find suitable employment because all the jobs have been given to those with special connections?

What happens to people who have no say whatsoever in how their governments are run and are treated like cattle, if not worse?

What happens to people who have to live under the deadly shadows of drones?

What happens to a person who witnesses their entire family get wiped out by a 'precise' missile strike?

Desperate for belonging in my teenage years, these are the only people I have ever felt an affinity towards, and so as they radicalized, I radicalized with them.

Bush's 2003 invasion of Iraq and its resulting massacre of hundreds of thousands of innocent Iraqis represented the crossing of the "Rubicon" for me. You can pretty much draw a straight line from there to my arrest in 2006.

How does it feel to be radical?

You feel worthy, righteous, and heroic. You see yourself as a saviour of your people. Your mind obsesses over the injustices that they endure, and it eventually becomes the only thing you wish to talk about. You see the world in strictly black-and-white terms. Deep inside, you suspect that there may be other colours, and this subconsciously drives you to engage in a constant re-enforcement of your beliefs. It is said that those who are the most dogmatic are usually the least certain. A vivid depiction of this internal struggle is that of a boy who is perpetually fortifying the walls of a sandcastle he built too close to the waves.

When I arrived at the Special Handling Unit (SHU), I desperately tried to engage with the rehabilitative process, but sadly, the administration appeared uninterested, even disdainful at times. Feeling deeply rejected once again caused my radical ideology to reassert itself, leading me to become more extreme in the SHU than I ever was on the outside. Soon thereafter, I adopted a rebellious attitude towards the administration and refused to meet my parole officers for several years.

This state of affairs continued until ISIS declared its Caliphate, and news of its atrocities began streaming in. Before the rise of ISIS, when innocent people were killed, I would rationalize it as 'collateral damage' if the victims were non-Muslims or dismiss it as a 'mistake' when they were Muslims. Every atrocity committed by ISIS was like a tsunami that would violently demolish my sandcastle, leaving no trace of it behind. Yet, I kept frantically rushing back to rebuild it.

Eventually, the hideousness of this group led me to periods of depression that followed every massacre. At the time, I did not see my radical ideology as separate from my religion, which caused me to fear that abandoning it would lead to abandoning my faith. I also feared confronting the reality that I may have thrown my entire life away and brought so much suffering upon my family for no good cause.

Accepting the truth is not easy...

Holding on became harder and harder until it finally became impossible, and I simply had to let go out of sheer disillusionment. Surprisingly, what followed was not a free fall into a dark abyss of disbelief, but rather a spiritual ascent that is best captured in a poem I wrote called "Servant of the Ever-Merciful."

If you are not as beautiful as the sun,
when it spreads its light,
upon the face of lands and seas.

If you do not glow as the full moon does,
amid darkness,
illuminating the way for life's travellers.

If you are not as graceful as the lofty clouds,
spreading shade over life's scorched inhabitants,
raining water upon their parched lips,
bringing life to their dead lands,
then, I am afraid,
you have misunderstood,
what it means to be,
a servant of God.

I felt liberated to finally be able to see the world in its true colours. This feeling only intensified as I slowly took the shackles off, one by one. This process began a few years ago and has been ongoing ever since.

How do I view my experience?

Despite its hardships and painful losses, I see it as a blessing. Sometimes, I tell myself that I am acquiring a Ph.D. in Life Studies from the University of the Incarcerated. My life is meaningful despite the steel bars and the barbed wire fences. My future is bright. I know that. And to God, I am ever grateful for everything I've endured.

I ask the Canadian public to forgive me for betraying their trust and welcoming arms.

I ask the Muslim community to forgive me for causing them so much apprehension by being one of too many who have cast them under a dark cloud of suspicion.

I ask my dear parents to forgive me for breaking their hearts.

I ask my brother and sister to forgive me for causing them so much sadness and distress.

I ask my former wife—whose loss I have never recovered from—to forgive me for abandoning her and devastating her in such a way.

I ask her entire family to forgive me for turning their lives upside down. I ask all the young men who became involved because of me to forgive me for everything.

I ask their families for forgiveness, as well.

Last but not least, I ask my beloved daughter to forgive me for leaving her without a father.

Princess, when I see you in my dreams, I sometimes hold you in my arms and weep, and weep, and weep 'till I awake.

Beloved, knowing what I know now, if I could go back in time to be with you, I would be there in a heartbeat.

But grieve no more, for I once heard that the truth shall set you free...

And now

And now, after far too long

The truth runs through my veins.

Nightmares and Daydreams

This is my first night in prison. It's past midnight, and I'm in solitary confinement. The lights are permanently on, and I'm sitting on my bed—a thin, beige cot atop a grey slab of concrete—with my back against the wall. I'm looking straight ahead, but my mind is elsewhere.

My life has just been shattered into a million pieces, now floating around the room like space debris. Now begins the task of trying to piece them together.

Some pieces are lost forever.

The only glue I have is *truth*,

but I don't know that yet ...

∞

When you enter a place like this, *dignity* is something you leave at the front door. This is the tenth time I've been strip-searched this week.

∞

This is my third year in solitary confinement. It's past midnight, summer is here, and there's been a blackout for the last two days. The ventilator has stopped breathing and the air is heavy and rotten.

I wonder if I'll make it.

∞

A man's face has just been cut open by two vicious razor swipes.

He's only 26-years-old, but he's scarred for life.

So am I.

And so is everyone else here.

Welcome to Maximum Security.

∞

We're on lockdown.

Again.

Living in a Maximum Security prison is like being inside the bowels of someone who is chronically constipated...

Movement is rare.

∞

His enemy is secure, for now, behind a solid steel door with a small plexiglass window. As he stealthily approaches the door, he quickly squats and takes out two plastic bottles that contain what appears to be muddy water. Attached to the lids of each bottle are yellow plastic tubes designed to give whatever is launched out of them a 45° trajectory.

Still squatting, he places the bottles at the bottom of the door and quietly slides their yellow cannons through the open crack.

The Trojan Tails are in!

Grinning from ear to ear, he then quickly stands back up and reveals himself to his enemy through the small window as he stomps on both bottles, causing liquid shit to explode into the cell.

The victory is swift, total, and undeniable.

Just par for the course in the Special Handling Unit.

∞

I'm in our tiny laundry room, lying on a metal footlocker. Two lifers across from me are bickering about whether Inuit children have televisions in their igloos.

Water is dripping on my forehead from the ceiling. It could be water leaking from the toilets upstairs, but I'm not concerned.

Do Inuit children have televisions in their igloos?

∞

The man across from me washes his bedding every day (sometimes twice); a severe case of OCD with more than a dash of Paranoid Schizophrenia.

Yesterday, he told me that his bed smelled like shit.

Today, the laundry machine is broken.

How will he survive?

∞

It's 11:05 a.m.

I'm standing at the crack of my door, watching the guard delivering mail. I'm all the way at the end. Will he make it here, or will he turn around just before he gets to my cell?

I pray for a letter... *for proof that I exist.*

He's definitely approaching my cell.

My heart skips a beat.

I run to my bed and sit there facing the wall, pretending as if I'm oblivious to his existence.

He's in front of my door now, rummaging through papers and envelopes.

My hopes skyrocket.

He drops something on my hatch and leaves.

They have now surpassed the moon!

I perform a supernatural leap towards my door and spot a folded paper. Not an envelope.

My rocket crashes back to Earth.

I open the folded paper.

It's just our biweekly account statement.

Try again tomorrow.

THIS PLACE

Snakes lurk in this place.
They are all highly venomous;
leave no skin exposed.

This place is very cold.
Your soul shivers and trembles;
only faith can warm it.

This place is very dark.
Eyes of the head malfunction here;
insight is required.

This place is very sad.
Joy is considered contraband;
learn to smuggle it.

This place clips your wings.
It fills your lungs with despair;
fly on the wings of hope.

BENEATH THE COMETS

"God does not play dice with the universe." - Albert Einstein

Bright red comets
streaking through the night sky
like a magic spell,
unleashed...

While I stand alone,
shivering to the bone,
on this cold night,
wondering...

In this darkness,
In this empty space,
In the vastness of my soul,
echo...

Why am I here?
For a purpose?
Or just a game of dice?

The Golden Nut

Clink clink clink clink DUFF!

I woke up startled as I looked ahead and saw a blurry vision of a man resembling Officer Hadfield standing at my cell door.

"Good morning, Amara. Sorry to wake you up this early, but the warden wants to see you in the yard."

Still alarmed and half-asleep, I looked towards my clock, which read 4:00 A.M.

"Am I in trouble?" I asked nervously.

"Not that I'm aware of."

"Alright, just give me a minute, please."

"Take your time."

I got dressed, brushed my teeth, and then walked out with him.

"When are you getting out of here, Amara?" he asked as we made our way down the empty corridors.

"I don't know. When are *you* getting out of here? Serving a life sentence on the installment plan?" I asked teasingly, as the anxious adult in me went to sleep and my inner child took charge.

He chuckled and asked, "What would you do if you ever got out?"

"I would go back to the desert, marry 22 wives, and live off camel meat and goat milk for the rest of my life. Every year, I would father 11 boys and 11 girls; each batch of kids would form a soccer team that would train together until they became good enough to compete in the Olympics. Then—"

"Seriously!" he interjected, barely containing his laughter.

"I don't know! I don't even know what I'll do tomorrow!"

"Fair enough," he conceded.

Sometimes, you have to verbalize people's cartoonish stereotypes to make them realize just how ridiculous they really are.

We finally approached the door that led to the yard. Mrs. Collins was standing there waiting for us.

"Good morning, Mr. Amara!" she said with an orchestrated smile that struggled to maintain its form.

"Good morning. What's this about?" I asked.

"Follow me," she said as she opened the door that led to the outer yard.

What I saw next was beyond incredible. Imagine a prison yard as big as a football field, illuminated by floodlights, with a soaring mountain at its center, made up entirely of millions and millions of chestnuts.

"Are you okay, Mr. Amara?" she asked as I stood there in sheer awe of what I saw before me.

"*What is this?*" I whispered in absolute awe.

"At the end of every millennium, a portal opens up in the upper stratosphere and rains down millions of chestnuts upon a single location. A golden nut is hidden in one of the chestnuts. Whoever keeps it in their possession can never die," she explained, sounding more like a witch than a warden.

"Cool. So why did you call me?"

"Because these chestnuts won't crack open unless the one doing the cracking is of Middle Eastern descent."

Why am I not surprised?

"So, you want me to crack nuts!" I said with a big grin.

"Not everything is a joke, Mr. Amara."

"Sorry, I just can't help myself sometimes. So, what will I get out of this? I mean, this could potentially take a very long time."

"Freedom," she whispered as if casting a spell.

The choice before me was obvious, so I accepted.

"Excellent," she said as she handed me a nutcracker and wished me good luck.

I then walked towards the bottom of the mountain, where a stool was waiting for me. I still thought this entire exercise was hilarious. I imagined the headline: "Zakaria Amara, the man who cracked a billion nuts to earn his freedom," as I sat down and began cracking away.

But after a while, it wasn't so funny anymore. My mood grew sombre as memories of my past along with hopes for my future flashed before me. I went on labouring for a long time, barely taking any breaks to eat or sleep. Seasons changed; rain, wind, snow, and scorching heat. Days turned into weeks, weeks into months, months into years, and years into nothing. All the while, the night endured as it always does behind these walls.

I could sense myself growing old as my hair and beard turned long and grey. My hands began to tremble, and my body ached with pain. God only knows how much time had passed.

Everything has an end, even time itself.

One day, I finally collapsed to the ground and lay there, knowing I was only a few breaths away from the world to come. As I lay there, a nightingale landed near my head and stood by, looking at me as if waiting to hear my final words.

I have always wondered what a man thinks about in his final moments. I was not afraid of God, for I have always longed to meet Him. I felt comforted by the fact that my family knew that I loved them all with everything that I had, that I had given them the greatest gift that a human being could give to another in this life. But there was one person who I had let down in ways that I could not mend. In my final moments, I wished that I could tell my first love that I had never stopped loving her, even now, as my heart was beating for the last time. And with that wish, I uttered the words that every Muslim is taught to say before leaving this world:

There is no god but God

and Muhammad is His Messenger.

What does a teardrop mean at the end of a man's life?

I felt my soul depart as the nightingale fluttered its tiny wings and flew towards the heavens, singing its sacred song.

PURPOSE

O One who made this universe,
and gave each one their own purpose.
I sought you out throughout my life,
in every valley and every height,
in every secret cave on land,
in every trace of you, I found,
up in heaven and on the ground,
I call on you, broken.

My tears ascend towards the sky,
I'm filled with pain that is no lie,
my life is hard; I can't deny,
I'm reaching my limits.

I journeyed on for all these years,
wiping away my lonely tears,
withstanding pain and piercing fears,
for only one purpose.

If all of those who are on land,
and those in heaven or beneath the sand,
or in the oceans and seas you made,
had turned away from me with hate,
and all I had was a loving glance,
from you to me and a second chance,
achieved is my purpose.

DON'T SHOOT YOURSELF, HEMINGWAY

Don't shoot yourself, Hemingway.
Every day,
we're moving away,
this is no place to stay.
Memories fading in the wind,
like autumn leaves.
Loss after loss,
it's a losing game.

"Life breaks everyone," you said,
and then we grow stronger
in all the broken places.
So many faces
that time erases.
Yet this can't be for nothing;
there is no need to rage against the dying of the light.
Be good.
Have faith.
For life is just a hallway,
and death is just a door.

WOUNDED BIRDS

On my first anniversary of incarceration, I walked into a rectangular, concrete yard with high walls. The yard was empty, except for a pigeon with a broken wing in a state of absolute panic. It was trapped in a frantic cycle—bursting upwards into flight, crashing into the wall, falling to the ground, and then repeating the pattern... and again... and again.

Someone had left breadcrumbs all around it, but it showed no interest in eating.

At that moment, I so badly wanted to say, "Why don't you calm down, nourish yourself, and allow your wounds to heal? You will never be able to fly again if you continue like this."

At that moment, staring at the bird felt like staring in a mirror.

We sometimes act like wounded birds,
flapping our broken wings to fly,
to fly away as we always do,
when we must stand in our truth.
When we must allow our wounds to heal,
when we're called on to be:
the truest versions of ourselves,
the souls we're meant to be.

LIFE PLAN

My hopes are now homeless
at the shelter of broken dreams.
I'm not happy,
this was not the plan,
not my youthful fantasy.
"Life is passing by,"
the mirror keeps on whispering,
"I love you," now rings hollow,
and no one seems to care.
This can't be my life.
So now, what is the plan?
Wither away in sadness?
like a flower in the fall,
like a prisoner in her chains,
like a dying, sick, old man,
Or,
Begin to change the seasons,
break the iron shackles,
and find eternal youth.

ANTHEM OF THE DARK NIGHT

Oh night of my soul, ever so dark!
Into your darkest corners, I shall embark.
Swimming through the deepest oceans of tears,
Withstanding the howling winds of my fears.
Seeking what every noble soul has sought,
A treasure that is neither sold nor bought!

If You Know How to Swim...

I might as well have been floating a million miles away from Earth, lost in outer space.
Moved from prison to prison.
Subjected to one catastrophe after another.
I was at my wit's end.
This was rock bottom.

It was my third year at the SHU; the nation's highest security prison, or Canada's deadliest fifty yards, as I preferred to call it.

Mentally, travelling back in time to retrieve these memories is not easy for me...

At the time, I had been in solitary confinement for several months. The vicinity echoed with shouts and a cacophony of loud noises, not to mention the self-mutilation and suicide attempts that were all too common, making madness a little too familiar in this place.

Thinking I could benefit from some silence in Ramadan, I volunteered to move to a stricter but quieter segregation unit.

Stereos and televisions were not allowed there. Even regular pens were considered contraband. Instead, we were issued a single rubber tube with an ink chamber inside it. These pens were nearly impossible to write with because they couldn't be held straight without bending.

But worst of all was the isolation, the suffocating concrete imposed silence, and the low incessant hum emanating from excessively bright fluorescent lights. Together, these forces conspired to chip away, hour by hour, at the very essence of what made me human.

With an appeal to my life sentence denied, freedom now seemed beyond even the land of dreams.

This was the closest I had ever gotten to being buried alive.

But there was one moment that I still vividly recall. It happened after two weeks in this extremely isolating place. I remember writing a letter to a friend, asking them to never write to me again. I just wanted to be left alone. Perhaps I believed that if I vanished physically and mentally from the lives of those who knew me, then I would somehow cease to exist altogether. But as I neared the middle of the letter, I felt as if a physical crack was tearing through my psyche.

Alarmed at this frightening sensation, I realized that I was now at the limits of my endurance. I had prided myself all along for prevailing despite all that was thrown my way, but at that moment, I knew that I was teetering on the perilous edge of sanity. This was it.

Zak... you can't do this to yourself anymore.
You just can't!
Listen to me...
Listen...
You can't allow yourself to drown...
if you know how to swim!

An epiphany...
An awakening...
A shift in thinking...
Something akin to being shocked back to life in an emergency room.

It was at that moment when I realized that I couldn't escape my destiny—that I must fight to survive so long as my heart was beating.

So, from the depth of that dark sea, I began to make my way upwards, even though I could see no surface.

A few days later, I found myself standing in prayer at night. The room was dark, but light was beginning to flicker in my heart. I remember talking to God and sensing that I was intently being listened to. I remember feeling a warm embrace around me. I remember sensing that I would one day be *here*.

That night may have been the Night of Destiny Muslims famously seek in the last ten nights of Ramadan. That, I am not certain of, but what I do know for sure is that my destiny began to shift after that night.

You can't allow yourself to drown
if you know how to swim.
Pushed to the furthest limits
now returning.
Emerging from the haunting darkness
reborn and unburdened.
Old skins shed
and past lives forgotten.
A slow drum beat
echoes through the silence.
As light cracks through,
revealing my new form.
Tearful and smiling,
broken and mended.
I am here...
I am here...

HOPE

I Remember a Time...

This is one of my earlier poems. It captures an exercise I used to engage in while I was incarcerated at the Special Handling Unit, Canada's highest security prison. It's hard to convey to you in words what it was like to be there. "Horrific" and "hopeless" are two words that come to mind. *There*, freedom felt like something that belonged to a different universe. I remember waking up sometimes and imagining that I was sailing on a lonely boat in an infinite ocean. I would then stand on my bed and pretend to climb a mast. Once at the top, I would look to the north for signs of land:

"No, nothing there today."

Then, I would look towards the east, west, and south:

"Nope, nothing there either."

Then, I would climb back down and say—half disappointed but also half hopeful, "God willing, tomorrow I will try again..."

∞

I remember a time not long ago
when I once sailed all alone.
When despair was an endless ocean
and the land of hope was but a dream.
When I would awake at the break of dawn
and the highest mast I would slowly climb
to look for as far as my eyes could see,
hoping for an end to my misery.
My sight would return with nothing at all,
my heart would ache as my head would fall.
But in my sadness, I would hear a voice,
Saying despair was but a choice.
You're not alone, for God is your friend,
and every hardship must one day end.

How to Overcome a Life Sentence

How do you wrap your head around the fact that you have been sentenced to spend the rest of your life behind bars? How do you free yourself from the chokehold of this giant? One loose enough to keep you from dying, yet tight enough to prevent you from living?

For many years, I have fought this monster using different swords. Every time one broke, a new one needed to be forged. I remember the first weapon I used against it was trying to convince myself that being in prison was better for my soul than being free. I often used to quote the Soviet prison camp survivor, Aleksandr Solzhenitsyn, who wrote:

"And anyway, would you yourself want freedom after so many years; would you want to go outside into the frenzied whirl, so inimical to the human heart, so hostile to the peace of the soul? Would you not pause on the threshold of your prison and peer anxiously out; should I or shouldn't I go there?"

Indeed, prison has many virtues. It is a place where you can meditate over the deepest questions of life, a place where you can form a very real relationship with your Creator. Prison is an alchemic environment that can transform your soul into gold or lead, *depending on your attitude*. Victor Frankl once wrote:

"We who lived in concentration camps can remember the men who walked through the huts comforting others, giving away their last piece of bread. They may have been few in number, but they offer sufficient proof that everything can be taken from a man but one thing: the last of human freedoms – to choose one's attitude in any given set of circumstances, to choose one's way."

This was a very powerful weapon that lasted a long time, yet it eventually wore down and shattered. A new approach was needed for which I had forged a new sword; one built on the idea that "to live is to suffer." I said to myself that suffering is a reality of life no one can escape. People out there diagnosed with terminal illnesses or facing a calamity with no end in sight feel exactly as lifers do. It works well when you're in the eye of the storm but offers no way forward once the winds subside.

I once again was reminded of Solzhenitsyn, who wrote:

"However clever and seemingly irrefutable such philosophical systems as skepticism or agnosticism or pessimism may be, you must remember that they are in their very nature condemned to impotence. They cannot govern human activity because people cannot stand still, and so cannot do without systems that affirm something, that point to some destination."

I needed to discover the missing element, whose absence caused the previous two swords to break. After a long period of introspection, I came to realize that while both approaches were based on solid truths, *a spirit of despair animated them*. Take, for example, the approach of telling myself that being in prison was better than being free and enumerating all the very real virtues of incarceration. What drove this approach was the subconscious despair of ever being free. No matter how many philosophical and spiritual arguments we could come up with, there's something in our very being that yearns for freedom. As for despair, it is a poison that slowly eats away at our souls and spreads throughout our bodies until we finally lose the will to live. Its ultimate manifestation is suicide, but it all begins once we give up on *hope* and choose to despair.

It took me eleven years to finally realize what hope actually meant. I used to think that maintaining hope was only possible when a glimmer of light could be seen in the distance, giving you the flimsiest reason to hold on to, but a reason nonetheless. But that's not what hope is about. Hope is most real when there is no light at the end of the tunnel. Hope is most real when you see no land on the horizon but instead see oceans stretching infinitely in every direction. Hope is most real when you have no tangible reason to hope.

The Prophet Muhammad (peace be upon him) once said:

"If the final hour of this world arrives and one of you has a sapling in their hand, then let them plant it."

The act of planting a tree in the dying moments of this world is one of the greatest acts of hope imaginable. With this in mind, it's crucial that we live our lives with hope. We must wake up every single morning hoping that somehow, something will happen that will bring joy to our lives. It may be something as small as a letter from a loved one or as big as the wonderful news that you might be free again. With hope, nothing is impossible.

Having realized all this, rays of hope burst forth from my heart, illuminating everything in sight. The monster's cold hands began to warm up, and his grip began to loosen. He let go of me, but as he turned to leave, he paused for a moment and said, "A thousand of your swords could do no harm to me. On the despair of souls I feed; you are no longer of use to me."

On that day, I thanked God for His deliverance and wrote these verses:

I remain hopeful,
Even when I see no reason to be.
The walls are high as heaven.
The doors are sealed shut.
Darkness envelopes me in layers,
yet the sapling of hope is in my right,
and I dare to plant it...
Knowing the world might end tonight.

GENTLE RIVER

My body dwells within a hopeless tomb,
while my spirit soars beyond the fullest moon.
Where my journey takes me, I shall go,
like a peaceful, gentle river, I do flow.
My heart is free of any expectations,
no room remains for plans or reservations.
The rhythm of my hope beats like a drum,
for I believe the best is yet to come.

THE WALL OF WHERE

While travelling through the mazes of my soul,
I came across a giant crystal wall.
Its surface glittered like a summer sea,
and deep within it lay a golden key.
I took one step closer to the wall,
and that's when I heard the caller's call:
"Do not obsess with tomorrow's *where*,
but *who* you are when you're finally there."

LIFE SURFER'S ANTHEM

I shall ride the waves of life;
the rough and the smooth,
until the very end.

I shall not despair when I crash,
nor be exuberant when I find myself upon the highest tide.

I shall ride through the storms,
through the vicious winds,
through the overwhelming darkness.

I shall ride through the sunny days,
beneath the open sea-blue skies,
as the gentle breath of God renews my soul.

I shall ride the waves of life,
always moving forward.

My destiny propels me to the finish line,
who can stop the hands of time?

LET IT BE SAID

Helen Keller lost her ability to hear and see after catching scarlet fever as a toddler. In one of the most moving passages in her autobiography, she writes about how grateful she was for being able to touch a tree and still remember what a tree looked like...

Her story inspired me to write this poem.

∞

When the stars give out...
And the moon says goodnight,
for one last time,
and the curtains close,
and no more days are left behind,
then let it be said...
then let it be said that you were grateful,
for this life,
for this miracle,
for this unlikely journey.
for every ray of sunshine,
for every planted seed,
for every shoulder cried on,
and every smile received.

Helen Keller – image reconstruction based on archival
photos made with Midjourney AI

BURIED TREASURE

Come, take a rest.
You've been a juggler all your life.
Isn't it time to let your thoughts fall?

Chains can never last forever,
but buried treasures sometimes do.

Sometimes I feel like I'm sitting
at the bottom of an ocean
chained and shackled
yet somehow, I'm not drowning.

There is a buried chest,
within my chest
and it contains a heavy cloak of sadness;
In there is a dancing clown, too:
a demon,
and an angel,
a gentle scented breeze,
and a giant tree whose leaves of love are always falling.
God is in there, too,
and so are you.

NEAR AND DEAR

The Arabian Night

ACT 1:
THREE WISHES

I entered my cell at around 8:15 p.m. last night. Seconds later, the steel door behind me slowly started to close itself shut:

Clink clink clink clink Clunk!

I despised that sound. Once, I had glued grey strips of sponge across the entire edge of the door, hoping it would mute this awful noise, but it was all in vain.

Clink clink clink clink Clunk!

If failure had a child, that's exactly what it would sound like. Anyhow, weekend nights in prison were incredibly boring, especially without a television. Mine was still with Andy, my Scottish 78-year-old neighbour. I gave it to him as a gift when I noticed he didn't own one, so I guess I couldn't call it *mine* anymore.

I looked outside my window and saw nothing but night and snow. So, with nothing better to do, I turned to my desk and began to write.

A few seconds later, *PUFF!*

I could see in my peripheral vision a fat, blue genie hovering in the air in front of my door. I paid no attention to him and continued writing; such surprise night visitations don't startle Middle Easterners.

As expected, using a thick accent, he offered me the customary three wishes.

I rolled my eyes and continued to scribble away. I was playing hard to get. I had to! Every Middle Eastern kid knows what happens when you show too much eagerness to a genie.

He repeated his offer.

Still looking down at my desk and sounding deeply annoyed, I said: "Give me a minute! I need to think about it!"

Filled with bottled excitement, I thought about my wishes. I thought about freedom. I thought about being reunited with my beloved daughter. I thought about my wonderful sister who had been my rock. I thought about my mother, father, and brother.

I thought about having all the money in the world.

I thought about being eternally young.

But then...

But then, I thought about the journey I've been on. Despite all the pain, all the fear, and all the tears... despite the loneliness... despite being turned into an outcast... despite all this, I thought about the wonderful treasures my heart has gained. I thought about all the knowledge and wisdom I picked up along the way. I thought about how my character has been shaped and moulded by the passing of the years... and finally, I thought about all the other treasures that still await me and how I would miss out on them if I simply abandoned my journey.

I looked hard at the paper on my desk for a moment and then reached for the light switch and retired to my bed.

I'm not sure if the genie bothered to take a look at what I wrote after I fell asleep. But if he did, then he would have read this:

"Ancient wisdom teaches that the arrival of a good thing before its time spoils it."

ACT 2:
THREE STRIKES

Clink clink clink clink DUFF!

No clunk this time. When the door opens, it's just *DUFF*. I like *DUFF*! It's gentler and more promising. Unless, of course, a bunch of guys are waiting to stab you on the other side, then *CLUNK* is definitely preferable.

It was 7:30 p.m. at night. Yard and gym activities were scheduled to begin two hours ago. I was ready as usual with my white fishnet sack that contained everything I needed for my outing. I usually took my prayer mat, workout pads, and a ball cap.

As I left my cell, I noticed that all the other cell doors were closed. Was I the only person going out to the yard tonight? *The Bachelorette* must be on, I thought. I left my living unit and proceeded through the seemingly endless and shifting corridors. At the end of one of the shorter hallways, I noticed Officer Robinson waiting for me. Judging from the two golden stripes on his shoulders, I figured he was the one in charge tonight.

A significant number of prison guards—if not the outright majority—classify inmates as a sub-human species. Mr. Robinson belonged to the minority; he was one of those people whose presence resurrected your faith in the universality of human decency.

As I approached him, he greeted me and asked how I was doing. His inquiry was genuine. I told him that I was fine and asked him what he needed. As he began to speak, I noticed a mixed expression of embarrassment and discomfort on his face:

"Amara, in the next hour, the U.S. President will declare his WWBYWWFY policy."

"What's WWBYWWFY ?" I asked.

"It stands for: 'We'll Bomb You Wherever We Find You.' It's a new global military campaign that will target anyone, anywhere, even if they happen to be on U.S. friendly soil like Canada."

"So, what does that have to do with me?"

"Corrections Canada believes that due to the vague and broad language of this policy, there is a possibility you may become a target of a drone strike while you are out in the yard. So, they want you to sign this waiver to absolve them of any responsibility."

I don't know why, but I've always found signing documents irresistible. I'm like a crackhead when it comes to the dotted line. If I see it, I must sign it. So, sign I did. Mr. Robinson stood there silently; he seemed to be still struggling with all of this.

As I walked away, I heard him ask, "Aren't you afraid?"

I turned towards him and said: "I am, but there is an Arabic poem that comes to mind:

"Die by the tip of a sword
or the tip of a slipper;
The causes of death are many,
but death itself is one."

I was tempted to change the end of the first line to "The tip of a Hellfire missile," but he would've probably called me out on my B.S.

I kept it moving until I finally reached the central control area, and walked through the metal detector. Its purpose was to prevent inmates from bringing shanks to and from the yard. Finally, the last corridor! I could see the light at the end of the tunnel!

"AA-MERAA!" The guard manning the metal detector called out from behind his counter.

My attention shifted from the thought of possibly getting drone-struck to the guard, who appeared to be holding a large, glazed doughnut in his left hand. Upon closer inspection, I realized that it was just a plastic replica that was attached to the end of his key chain. I don't mind doughnuts.

"Three strikes!" he said with a bulldog expression on his face. "You can't go to the yard tonight. Try again tomorrow." There was satisfaction in his voice.

I have a triple black belt in conflict avoidance and a white belt in self-esteem, so I politely turned towards him and asked, "What did I do wrong?"

"Well, Aa-mera, according to the new regulations, Maaa-zlim inmates are no longer allowed to take their prayer mats to the yard."

"Why?"

"They're a flight risk."

"But this is not the flying type," I politely protested.

"Can the naked eye distinguish between which is which, Aa-mera?"

He got me there!

"Can't argue with you on that one, Sir."

"Secondly, all inmates are now prohibited from keeping beards that are longer than .765433 cm. Long beards could be used to hide weapons and other contraband."

"And what's the third infraction?"

"The administration has decided that you specifically are no longer allowed to wear shoes to the yard. This shouldn't be a big hassle for you since I see you camel jockeys wearing slippers in the desert all the time."

"Your information about our footwear is very accurate, but why am I specifically not allowed to wear shoes?"

He reached under his counter and pulled out a gigantic 3-ring black binder that was labelled "Unknown Unknowns." When he opened it wide on his counter, I noticed that it contained nothing. Yet, to my astonishment, he began to sift through it as if it were full of documents. He shifted back and forth, and at some point, even licked the tips of his finger to separate between two invisible pages that were apparently stuck together.

"Aha!" he exclaimed when he finally found what he was looking for, and began to read:

"It says here: 'There is *unknown unknown* evidence that indicates Mr. Aa-mera has previously formulated an escape plan, and could potentially execute it when he feels the time is right.'"

PAUSE ||

My mind scrambled through my memories like a fighter jet seeking a target. How did they find out?! And which plan exactly are they talking about?

For one, there was that first night in prison when I fantasized about turning into an ant-sized version of myself and then crawling beneath the door. This was a completely original idea. I honestly had no clue at the time that Ant-Man even existed.

Oh! I think I know... Years ago, when I was at Canada's Super Max, a great idea came to me as I was walking in the yard with another inmate. I suggested to him that if he ran around the yard for 30 minutes every day while flapping his arms like a bird, then eventually, after a very long time, he might grow feathers and fly his way to freedom. He pointed out that the snipers in the towers might shoot him down. I told him it was worth a shot!

Darn it. They must have overheard us. Or maybe, instead of transforming into an elegant bird, he simply took the path of least resistance, and devolved into a tail-dragging rat!

Can't trust anyone these days.

PLAY ▶

Humour has always been my way of coping with hardship. The harder my life gets, the funnier I get. I remember going back to the holding cells after receiving a life sentence and launching into a series of jokes about how I would deal with it. The truth is that I was hurting *then*, just as I was hurting *now*.

"Alright, Sir. I guess I'll try again tomorrow."

I felt dejected, lowered my head in defeat as I left the central control area, and walked through the corridor that led back to my living unit.

PUFF!

Suddenly, the opportunistic, blue genie appeared in front of me.

"I offer you three wishes!" he announced with clear satisfaction in his voice, now that he thought I was desperate.

I looked at him with my sad eyes for a moment, and then simply walked past him.

After a few steps, I heard him repeat his offer again.

I stopped without turning and said, "My only wish is that we can all one day see ourselves in each other."

The genie instantly disappeared, never to be seen again...

ACT 3:
THREE POINTER

I was in the prison gym one night, shooting hoops. I couldn't play anymore. I could only shoot—back problems at 33... or was it 34? Honestly, at that moment, I wasn't entirely sure. Believe it or not, I spent most of my 31st year thinking that I was 32 years old until my actual 32nd year arrived, and I realized my mistake. I felt frustrated when I discovered this because it meant that I had to mentally think of myself as a 32-year-old for two years in a row.

I could easily do the math and figure out my current age, but for some reason, I'm allowing the uncertainty to stick around like a half-welcomed squatter. (Definitely a topic for therapy!)

Anyway, I'm a decent three-point shooter. A few years ago, I was one of the best in the building. I won the three-point competition twice, and even used to walk around the gym with an invisible championship belt until I (invisibly) put it on the line and lost it to a man named T. I desperately tried to win it back from him before he was released, but I just couldn't beat him. I wonder what he did with it. After he left, I pretended to still have the belt, but it wasn't the same. You can only lie to yourself for so long, even if no one calls you out on it.

I'm digressing again.

Focus.

I saw the warden walking in my direction as I was shooting hoops. She never came to the gym, so her visit was definitely unusual and with a clear purpose in mind. Truthfully, I was trying extra hard to impress her, which led me to miss every shot.

"AMARA!" she yelled.

I tried to act cool despite my horrible performance and walked over to the sideline where she was standing.

"Yes, Mrs. Collins. What would you like?"

"How are you?" she asked without a trace of empathy.

"Just another day, Ma'am. What about you? You never come to the gym. What's up?"

"Well, I have an offer for you."

"Okay."

"If you manage to score the next three-pointer you take, we'll commute your life sentence, and you'll be a free man."

"That's funny," I said with my trademark 5% laugh.

"I'm serious. Here is the paperwork. Just sign over here if you agree." She pointed at the dotted line.

"What if I miss?" I asked.

"If you miss, then you'll have to enter the Environmentally Friendly Energy Initiative that we just started here at Millhaven Institution."

"What's that about?"

"It's a fantastic new method of producing environmentally friendly energy to power up the building, by harvesting it from the bodies of permanently unconscious inmates."

"You mean like The Matrix?"

"Exactly."

"Where do I sign?"

"Right here."

I already told you about me and dotted lines, so don't bother trying to figure out what I was thinking as I nonchalantly signed the document.

I grabbed the ball, headed to the top of the three-point line, and faced the net. Hit or miss, I was on the brink of freedom, or an unconsciously conscious existence in a dream world.

I did not stand there for an eternity, reflecting on my past, or my future, as one usually does in Hollywood movies. I simply looked at the net, measured the distance, jumped crookedly as I always do, and released the ball, sending it up into a perfect arc that took its time as it swam through empty space...

... until it finally landed perfectly on the warden's head. *Oops!*

I didn't have time to think about how I so completely missed the net, because I suddenly felt a sharp pain in my upper left arm. I instinctively grabbed my arm, and immediately noticed a syringe-looking dart sticking out of it. Forgive me for not knowing what this thing was called; I was born in the Middle East, and over there, they just shoot us. But maybe... Maybe if they developed their own Environmentally Friendly Energy Initiative, then things might change. Who knows?

I quickly began to fade, and my vision became blurry. The last thing that I saw was a guard standing on a window balcony, holding what looked like a rifle that was pointed in my direction.

Complete darkness.
Suddenly, my eyes opened.
My heart was racing, and I was gasping for breath.
I looked around frantically, trying to register my surroundings.
I was lying on a bed.
I looked towards my feet and saw a familiar steel door.
This was my cell.
Clink clink clink clink DUFF!
Breakfast time.

EPILOGUE

"They slept on two stories of the building, and on two-tiered bunks, and they dreamed; old men of their families, young men of women. They dreamed of lost possessions, a train, a church, their judges... Their dreams were all different, but whatever they dreamed, the sleepers were miserably aware that they were prisoners.

If in their dreams they roamed over green grass or through city streets, it could mean only that they had tricked their jailers and escaped or had been released in error and were now wanted men. That total, blissful forgetfulness of their shackles imagined by Longfellow in "The Prisoner's Dream" was denied them.

The shock of wrongful arrest, followed by a ten- or twenty-year sentence, the baying of the guard dogs, the sound of escort troops priming their rifles, the nerve-racking jangle of reveille in the camps, seep through all the strata of ordinary experience, through all their secondary and even primary instincts, into a prisoner's very bones so that, sleeping, he remembers that he is in jail before he becomes aware of smoke or the smell of burning and gets up to find the place on fire."

From Aleksandr Solzhenitsyn's "In the First Circle"

POEMS TO MY DAUGHTER...

Being in prison for all this time stripped me of the years I could have spent with my daughter. While entrapped between four walls, drowning in the echoes of a distant fight, screaming, or clanking on metal bars, I slipped into an oasis of my own—one where I am with her, holding her hand, embracing her tightly, and listening to her laugh. In this oasis, I wrote a series of poems to my daughter. A part of me hopes that they played some role in helping her grow into the beautiful young lady she is today. May God protect her and look after her now, just as He did when I was inside. Amen.

When I am Gone...

When I am gone, these words shall stay
for you to read at night or day.
In them, you'll find me urge you on,
declaring, "Darkness must end by dawn."
I missed the day you learned to walk
and your first words as you tried to talk.
When you were sick, I was not there
to hold you tight and give you care.
Seeing your friends in their dads' embrace
is a sin of mine I can't erase.
I was not there to wipe your tears,
a regret I've held for all these years.
Leaving you was my greatest crime
I wish I could turn the hands of time.
But now I'm here between each line,
sending my love with every rhyme.
These gems are a gift from me to you
always have hope, and always be true.

From this poem, a series of poems titled "The Gem Series" was born. These poems hold my entire heart, ripped straight from my chest and littered on these pages.

GEM #1: CHRYSOCOLLA
(Wisdom, Communication, and Gentle Power)

Beloved Princess,

I hope that you will take these gems and place them on your crown. For if you wish to be queen one day, you must prepare from now.

I'm still young,
yet old enough,
for I see signs of grey.
We one day came, and soon we'll go,
nothing remains the same.
At your age, not long ago, I thought I knew it all,
but now I know with certainty,
that I know nothing at all.

GEM #2: AQUAMARINE
(Calm, Centered, and Relaxed)

How often have you seen a man,
whose beauty brings delight,
yet whose ugly character,
makes you run with fright.
How often have you seen a girl,
whose looks are not so fine,
yet each word that leaves her lips,
makes the whole world shine.

GEM #3: ROSE QUARTZ
(Unconditional Love)

My Beloved Princess,

Know that I will always love you no matter what. You are perfect to me, and I accept you just as you are. There is nothing you need to do to gain my love; you already have it unconditionally.

You can fail in school a thousand times,
you can break my rules again and again,
you can crush my heart and bring me to tears,
but nothing you do will diminish my love.
With your tiny hands, you captured my heart,
and there it remained since the very start.

DAUGHTER OF THE WELL

"On the day when
the infant girl
who was buried alive
shall be asked,
for what crime was she murdered?" (81:8-9)

This verse from the Quran was revealed to rebuke the practice of some pagan Arabs who used to bury their infant daughters alive due to fear of shame and poverty. A man once approached the Prophet Muhammad (peace be upon him) and said: "O Messenger of God, I used to have a daughter...One day, I asked her mother to prepare her for a visit to her uncle's house. My daughter became very happy when she heard this, but my poor wife knew exactly what that meant. All she could do was weep and obey. When my daughter was finally ready, I took her out to a well and told her to look into it, and as she was doing so, I came from behind and kicked her forward...Her last words as she rolled down the well were: 'Daddy! Daddy!'"

Upon hearing this, the Prophet sobbed as if he had just lost a member of his own family.

I penned this poem in memory of that little girl...

How did it feel?
To fall, to roll, to drown,
to see your dad
as you turned around.

Which pain was worse?
The burning gasp for breath?
or the painful knowledge of
the cause behind your death?

METAMORPHOSIS

They said to her,
though a child she was,
Why were you ever born?!
She looked at them,
but could not speak,
so she began to crawl.
They said to her,
though a child she was,
Nothing you do is right!
She looked at them,
but could not speak,
so she began to run.
They said to her,
though a child she was,
We wish that you would die!
She looked at them,
but did not speak,
and instead began to fly.

DIAMOND IN THE FLAMES

Her life was drowning her in pain.
No more abuse could she sustain.
She took a match and lit it up,
hoping the pain would finally stop
The flames began to eat her dress,
for grievances that weren't addressed.
She knew that now the end was here,
her heart was thus consumed by fear.
So in her panic, she tried to shout,
when suddenly the flames went out,
and in the darkness, she saw a light,
then felt a breeze that brought delight.
She heard a voice from up above,
whose gentle tone was full of love,
that said to her, "my little girl,
you are to me a precious pearl.
I know that men can be so cruel,
like wolves with bloody fangs that drool.
I know that life can be so tough,
for you're a diamond in the rough.
One day, these wolves will pay the price
I'll trap them all like cowering mice
One day, you'll shine like a glowing star,
and all shall know who you are.
One day will come when you'll be free,
hold on to hope, for that's the key."

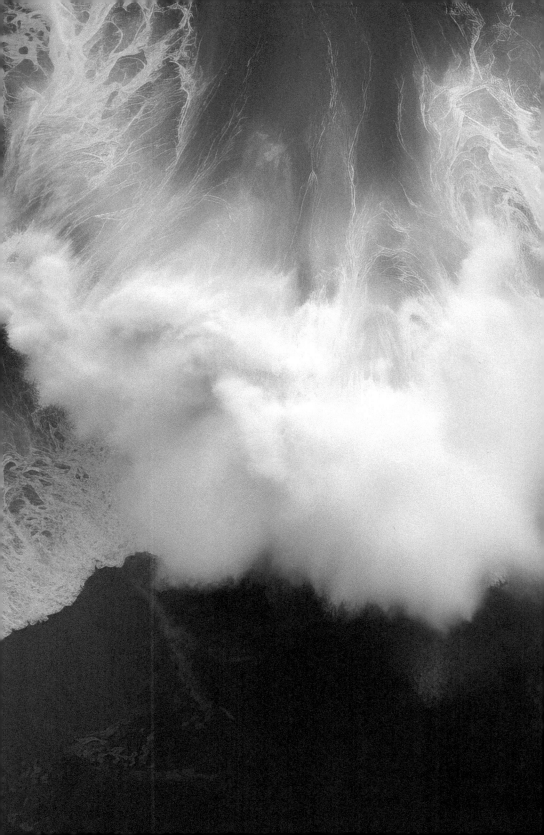

MEANING

In Search of Meaning

Some of us wake up and see nothing but rows upon rows of prison bars for as far as our mind's eye can see. On those days, we wonder whether we have forever lost the chance to make something of our lives. We look back and see nothing but a haunting past littered with shattered dreams. We look ahead and see nothing but a future as dark as a raven flying on a moonless night. We wonder whether our lives even matter anymore. It kills us to think that we achieved nothing significant, to think that our lives might be as worthless as the froth on the ocean's surface.

Rabbi Harold Kushner tells us:

"I believe that it is not dying that people are afraid of. Something else, something more unsettling and more tragic frightens us. We are afraid of never having lived, of coming to the end of our days with the sense that we were never really alive, that we never figured out what life was for."

We may not realize it, but the drive to seek a meaningful existence is as necessary as our need to breathe. Without air, our bodies die; without meaning, our souls die. In every one of us is a void that cries out to be filled. Those of us who sought to fill it by climbing the summits of fame, fortune, power, physical appetites, and even knowledge have all found themselves consumed by the very void they sought to fill. Mitch Albom, best-selling author, writes:

"There was a stretch where I could not have worked more hours in the day without eliminating sleep altogether. I piled on accomplishments. I made money. I earned accolades. And the longer I went at it, *the emptier I began to feel*, like pumping air faster and faster into a torn tire."

So how then do we attain a meaningful life? Is it possible for a prisoner to even contemplate such a goal? Rabbi Kushner tells us that we must first get rid of the illusion known as the "Grand Solution." He writes:

"Trying to find one Big Answer to the problem of living is like trying to eat one Big Meal so that you will never have to worry about being hungry again... We never solve the problem of living once and for all. We can only deal with it day by day, a constant struggle to fill each day's worth of meaning."

How can we achieve that? *By responding to the demands of the moment.* Whether you are free or serving the longest sentence ever handed to a human being... Every moment of *your* life beckons you to respond to it. The Prophet Muhammad (peace be upon him) said that on the Day of Judgement, God will say to a man: "O son of Adam, I became ill, yet you did not come to care for me!" The man will reply with astonishment: "O my Lord, how could I have cared for you when you are the Lord of all Creation?" God will respond, "Did you not know that my servant so and so became ill, yet you did not go and care for him? Indeed, had you gone and cared for him, you would have found me with him."

Therefore, *even in prison*, when you find a sick man, care for him. When you come across a hungry woman, share your food with her. When you see someone sad, make them smile. When you see tears flowing, gently wipe them. When you see fires of conflict raging, strive to extinguish them. And above all, when it is time to worship the One who brought you into existence, then humbly present yourself in gratitude before Him.

By fulfilling the rights of the Creator and those of His creation, our own need for meaning is inevitably fulfilled. Ironically, what we are seeking from an elusive distant dream is right before our very eyes. These simple acts of kindness and devotion are what the Qur'an calls *"eternal."* They take a transient moment that could have been wasted on a meaningless pursuit and transform it into an eternal memory that transcends time itself like a dove gracefully ascending ever higher towards the celestial realms.

Rabbi Jonathan Sacks, while referring to a parable given to Tolstoy, writes, "Once there was a traveller who, wandering in the steppe, sees coming towards him a ravening beast. To save himself, he climbs into a waterless well, but he looks down and sees at the bottom a dragon, its jaws open, waiting to eat him. He dare not climb out, and he dare not fall. So he clutches hold of a wild bush growing in a cleft in the wall of the well. This alone suspends him between the death awaiting above and below. But his hands grow tired. He feels he must soon let go. Then he sees two mice, one white, one black, gnawing at the roots of the bush. So, even if he manages to keep hold of the bush, it will break off, and he will fall into the mouth of the dragon. At that moment, he sees some drops of honey on the bush's leaves and reaches to lick them. That, says Tolstoy, is life.

The dragon is death, the white and black mice, our days and nights. And all our pleasures are no more than drops of honey on a bush that will soon give way."

Whether we are free or incarcerated, the clock is ticking for all of us, and life is far more fragile than we realize. Tomorrow is not promised to us but today is here, and it beckons us to respond to it. We *all* have the opportunity to live meaningfully. *"The sad sight of human life untouched by transcendence"* is what we manifest when we choose not to.

CANCER OF RESENTMENT

How could You be when all I see is suffering?
When all I see are orphaned children waiting for You and wondering.
How could You let their innocence be robbed away in darkness?
How could You let their blood flow in endless streams? It's madness!
How could You be when those who claim belief in You are faithless?
They walk around self-righteously with vanity—it's nonsense!
They play with blood as casually as they would with water.
The only thing that's on their mind when they awake is slaughter.
I rest my case, I end my speech, and now I sit in silence,
waiting on You to answer me if You exist, Your Highness.

I heard your words, I always do, and now here is the answer,
you're not the first, nor are the last, to have this common cancer,
that kills the hearts and blinds the eyes from seeing all the wisdom,
in all my works, in all my deeds, throughout my endless kingdom.
When I first made your father Adam, all the angels questioned:
"Will You create those who kill and spread evil corruption?"
They failed to overlook the many evil ones and see,
a few humble hearts whose very being is mercy.
They feed the poor, they help the weak, and heal the sick and wounded.
They wipe the tears, they mend the hearts, and act as I commanded.
They offer thanks and speak with words that are always tender,
and when they pray, they bow their heads in humble surrender.
Had every inch of Earth been filled with every kind of crime,
and one such soul remained behind; I would allow them time.
Can you not see that nothing could be without its other pair,
Without a north, there is no south, and such are good and evil.
I gave you all the will to choose and thus you chose to be,
and now you turn around and point your finger blaming Me...

Enchanting Universe

Grains of sand
Pebbles and stones
Drops of rain
Deserts and bones
Blades of grass
Suns and Moons
Ancient trees
Ice and dunes
Soaring mountains
Comets and stars
Flowing fountains
Venus and Mars
Enchanting Universe
One chance to give
One blessing, one curse
One life to live.

MYSTERY

Mystery: /ˈmɪst(ə)ri/. A religious truth known by revelation alone. (Merriam-Webster dictionary).

Here I stand,
between the two eternities,
of past and future tense
in a spec of time
Sublime.
I fear a bitter harvest,
so I stay awake at night,
planting seeds of every kind,
am I behind?
What is the purpose of our lives?
Think.
Is it to gather all the toys?
And he who has the most ones wins?
Or is it to build a house of cards,
Then see it scattered by the winds?
Whims.

So here I stand,
wondering,
pondering,
questioning,
looking to my origins,
in search of my destination.
Who am I?
What am I?
And who is it that I shall be?
Mystery...

THE LAND OF SILENCE

Escape into the vast wilderness of silence,
near the burning bush,
where you might hear the voice of God.
Tiring thoughts,
and fears,
and worries,
rambling on inside my mind have pushed me here,
where snowflakes fall with grace,
one by one,
upon the silent Mount of Sinai.

Don't you think it's funny?
All this running around,
All this hustle and bustle,
All this frantic madness for more.
For what?
For who?
And for when?

We've done well.
Our house of cards is finally built.
But wind is on its way.
This is not the time to build,
but to run while walking slowly,
towards the land of God,
where the only language spoken,
or heard,
is silence…

When All that Remains

What happens when your remembrance,
causes me to forget myself?
When my incessant thoughts cease,
and the mountain,
made of my jagged fears,
and shards of broken dreams,
crumbles?
What happens when your name,
echoes,
through the chambers of my inner selves,
shattering the mirrors of my delusions,
and unifying my many voices into one?
What happens when I cross the threshold of doubt,
when I leap beyond the barriers of space and time,
when all that remains,
is You,
and only You...

UNTITLED

Where are you running to?
    To whom?
I loved you the very first day I made you.

Where are you running to?
    To whom?
I loved you more than a mother could ever love her child.

Where are you running to?
    To whom?
I loved you more than mere words could mean.

Where are you running to?
    To whom?
I loved you more than you will ever know...

THE OASIS

I wrote this story in 2018 when I was at Millhaven Max. At the time, things were just beginning to turn around for me, only to suddenly fall apart in every way imaginable. And so, I turned to my pen, and for nearly a month, I was a man possessed. If there is a single story in this entire book that I can credit with saving my life, this would have to be it.

You have reached the Oasis.
I have been waiting for you.
And you have finally arrived.
Everything that is to come is already near.

I am Abu Nour, a life traveller like yourself.
I was lost in the desert and wandered for what seemed like an eternity.
And like you, I refused to believe that anything in this world, not even an infinite desert, could conquer my soul.

Look around you.
Can you see just how impossible our existence is? Everything that surrounds us is hostile to us, and yet here we are! Out of the chaos of the desert, the order of the Oasis somehow emerges.
Do you see the sapling you are standing next to?

Look at how small and fragile it is, yet this entire Oasis moves forward because of it! I often think to myself that it must have a sense of humour, for it only seems to perform its miracle when we are not paying attention to it.

What about demons?
Do you believe they exist?
No?

Then, who do you think was responsible for all of those awful thoughts that you had in the desert? All those piercing doubts; all those imaginary fears and worries that whipped you into an anxious frenzy; all those cruel voices that told you again and again that you were worth less than the dirt beneath your feet?

The three demons of despair are always standing behind you, and since they can't uproot the sapling themselves, they constantly whisper despairing thoughts to you, *hoping* that you uproot it yourself. Despair is a choice. No one can take your hope away from you—only you can give it up.

The first demon whispers awful thoughts to you about your future.
The second demon whispers awful thoughts to you about yourself.
And the last demon whispers awful thoughts to you about everyone else.
Once you've given up on all those things, what reason is there to go on living?

The meaning of my name?

Abu Nour means *Father of Light*. Nour Al Huda is my daughter's name.
It means "The Light of Guidance." In a way, Abu Nour could not have existed
before she came along, for by giving her that name, she gave me mine. And now,
whenever I am mentioned, she is mentioned, and whenever she is mentioned,
I am mentioned, too. Though we are apart, we remain inseparable, and *that* is
the power of love...

This is the Tree of Love. Love is what connects us to everything and everyone.

Why is one side of the tree missing?

Because we are all traveling through life in search of what can fill our missing
half. You see, we all need to love and be loved... To love ourselves and to have
ourselves love us back... To love our parents and to have them love us back... To
love our siblings and to have them love us back... To love our neighbors and to
have them love us back... To love our soulmates and to have them love us back...
To love our children and to have them love us back... To love all living things and

to have them love us back... And no love...and no love is greater than the love of our Maker, *the uncreated Creator.*

Every evil, every illness, every wound can only *be* when love is absent. To love another human being is to be so concerned about their well-being that you are constantly seeking to fill the voids you find within them, wishing to make them whole.

Come. Look over here.
These engravings on the tree were left behind by past travelers.

"Love is the whole, and we are the pieces."

And read this one over here:

"Love is the river of life in this world. Think not that ye know it who stand at the little tinkling rill, the first small fountain. Not until you have gone through the rocky gorges, and not lost the stream; not until you have gone through the meadow, and the stream has widened and deepened until fleets could ride on its bosom; not until beyond the meadow you have come to the unfathomable ocean, and poured your treasures into its depths – not until then can you know what love is."

I often come here to remember my beloved.
When I was lost,
I was not alone...

My soulmate was with me. We both hoped to survive the harsh journey together. But after years of travel with no end in sight, I told myself that if I ever felt her grip weaken, then I would let her go in peace without resistance. So, when that moment finally arrived, and I felt her hand loosen, I told her that I loved her... and let her go. *Love is sacrifice.*

I still see her in my dreams, but even there, I can't bring myself to speak to her. Maybe I am afraid of finding out that she no longer loves me. Or maybe I am afraid of discovering that she is no longer the same soul that I once loved. And so, through silence, my memories of her are left preserved. Or maybe I am simply practicing the most perfect form of love. Whoever engraved this message here knew exactly what that meant:

"*Perhaps providence had rightly wanted him to be a chaste witness to a beauty that he should never disturb. Was this not the manifestation of the most perfect love, such as he professed to his lady, loving from afar, renouncing the pride of domination? Is aspiration to conquest love?*"

Have you ever wondered how the act of love is at its core an act of faith, and how the act of faith is at its core an act of love?

This is the Tree of Faith, standing proudly at the center of the Oasis. During its formative years, it is delicate and fragile, yet it gains strength and stature with each virtuous act you undertake and every storm you weather. Eventually, it ascends to the heavens, establishing a profound connection with our Maker.

When you climb this tree, you can see further in the distance; if you climb a bit higher, you may even see glimpses of the unseen world. And while you are up there, you can look down and gain a better perspective on how things really are...

Who is our Maker?

Only you can answer this question, but I will tell you this much: Just as there is only one of you, there is only one of Him, and the fact that you exist is proof that He exists. Go back to a time when you could not utter a single word or understand it. Go back to the days of innocence and see the world anew, and then you will realize that what I said is true.

Can this tree be destroyed?

Yes, it can. You see, every traveller must one day confront the demons of darkness. Not long ago, they descended upon the Oasis in thousands, wearing dark cloaks and hoods that concealed their faces. They came from every direction with blinding sand storms under the cover of pitch-black clouds that resembled moving mountains.

When I saw them approaching, I quickly dug a hole and hid in it after covering its mouth with branches and leaves. From there, I watched with sheer terror as these demons invaded the Oasis and destroyed everything in their path with fire and fury.

When they finally reached the Tree of Faith, it refused to burn, so they began digging at its base, determined to uproot it all together.

After everything that I endured. After everything that I survived. There I was, huddled in a hole, cowardly watching everything be destroyed, as if it never was, as if it meant nothing. At that moment, I heard the voice of an old friend repeating an old piece of advice, *"Abu Nour! Why do you always run away from your troubles? Don't you realize that even if you were to fly to the moon, then there, too, they would find you?"*

As these words echoed within me, I saw the thread that weaved through my entire life. I saw myself running from my troubles, from my loved ones, from myself, and from life itself...

I finally saw the pattern,
I finally pulled the thread,
And that's when it happened...

Feeling a surge of newfound strength, I climbed out of my hiding place without hesitation and threw myself at the first demon I saw. As we both went down, the back of his head landed hard on a rock, which instantly rendered him unconscious. As I attempted to get off him, my face came within inches of his, and that's when I saw his face clearly for the first time...

There are some truths in this universe that upon contact with, can alter you, transform you; transfigure you; utterly change your very being.

You see...
The demon on that ground was not a demon.
He was a man...
And that man was me.

The edges of my old universe began to roll back like a scroll being folded, while a new universe began to unravel. Tears from my eyes fell into his open mouth, and with every drop, a gentle light began to shine forth from it. As I looked around, I saw the forces of darkness collapse to the ground one after the other. The light grew in brightness and intensity, spreading in every direction, as the overwhelming darkness began to retreat like a wounded animal.

You, too, will experience your own battle with darkness, and if you find a way to see through it—even if you stumble as you try—then you will emerge transformed.

Just remember that faith without wisdom is blind, while wisdom without faith is heartless.

Look ahead. Do you see it?

The water of this well never overflows, nor is it too shallow to be reached by hand. To be wise, you must always do what is right, in the right manner, at the right time.

Go ahead and drink from it.

You see, in the beginning, you simply had knowledge of this well. Then, you saw it with your own eyes. And then, finally, you drank from it yourself.

Wisdom can't *actually* be taught; it must be experienced. Can you place a fruit on a tree? Of course not! It must grow from within. Therefore, everything that you have learned so far will only serve you once your soul is ready to bear its fruits.

Do you see these blue butterflies flying around?

They are the butterflies of forgiveness. They help keep the Oasis cool and pleasant. If they were to disappear, the desert's scorching heat would invade this place, and everything in it would die.

Only you can nourish these butterflies. Would you like me to teach you how?

Before you fall asleep every night, take a moment to forgive every soul that ever hurt you, and then ask your Maker to inspire those whom you have hurt to forgive you. It's much more difficult than it sounds, but a wise man once said that *"forgiveness is a gift that we give to ourselves."*

Have you ever noticed how the first victims of the flames of anger and hatred are their carriers?

The sun is about to set, and the night will soon arrive. Come with me; there is one last thing that I want you to see.

We have reached the northern edge of the Oasis, and this here is the Tree of Reliance. It looks like a Willow tree that is about to fall over from the sheer weight that it has burdened itself with.

Look ahead to the north. Do you see those giant frightening shadows? They are an illusion created by the demons of fear. I know this, and yet they still fill me with worry and anxiety. Sometimes their sight cripples me with such fear that I stay frozen in place until the sun mercifully sets, the shadows disappear, and my fear melts away. This is why I often come to this tree and sit beneath its comforting shade. Here, I can finally lie down my burdens and place them in the hands of my Maker.

Do you know what the last lesson of the desert is?

It is engraved right here:

"What hit you was never meant to miss you, and what missed you was never meant to hit you. The Pens of Destiny have been lifted, and their ink has long dried."

This is the last lesson because it is the most difficult to master. Let go of your illusions of control and realize deep within *that what shall be will be*. Do what you can do, and to your Maker, leave the rest.

It is a paradox. How can we have free will and predestined fate existing at the same time? I can't explain it to you in words, but if you travel long enough, you will realize the truth of my words. Freewill and Fate are like twin horses that we ride standing, not knowing which is which, until the race is over.

Come. Let us sit under the tree and watch the sunset.

Do you want me to tell you what will happen tomorrow?

Tomorrow, if our Maker wills, the sun will rise, and you too will rise with it. But unlike the shining bright sun, your heart will be veiled by dark clouds of discontent. You will rise pretending as if you awoke to the wrong life, suspecting that while you were asleep, a mishap must have occurred in the realm of the souls and that you were somehow assigned someone else's fate.

You will remain in that state for weeks, perhaps months, and possibly years until a single moment of clarity arrives, during which you will come to realize that the truths you have discovered here are, in fact, life's greatest treasures, and that if this is where your journey has led you so far, then perhaps you were never lost after all.

It is precisely at that moment
when you will rise back to your feet
and begin to walk back to the sapling of hope,
where you will stand there waiting,
waiting there,
as I once waited for you.

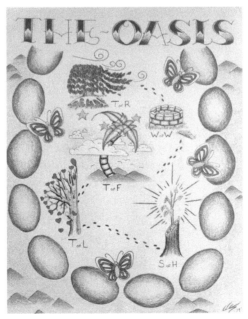

Illustrated by my friend and fellow prisoner,
Justin K.

Surviving the Dark Night of the Soul

It has been called the void, the abyss, the cave, the womb, and the dark night of the soul. Those who never experienced it can never fathom its reality, while most who are in its depths have no idea where they are. I was once trapped there for many years, but now I am slowly emerging.

Oh, how dark it has been!

I dedicate these words to someone who I care deeply about; someone who has just descended into its depths. I hope that she and others like her will find these pages and use them to make their way out. While still partially entrapped, I often stop to look back towards the center—towards a massive whirling cloud of menacing darkness—hoping to see a sign of her.

The void is not an evil place; it is a universal human experience. It sometimes manifests itself physically in the form of a prison, a cave, a whale, or a serious injury or illness. At other times, it manifests itself socially in the form of an unhappy relationship, the loss of a loved one, broken dreams, or the feeling of permanent entrapment beneath the rubble of wrong life choices. However, in all cases, the void is a psychological and spiritual struggle, an inner state that forces us to transform our inner selves or be forever condemned to languish in its depths.

In it, all the lies we lived are exposed, the games we played no longer function, and the stories we told ourselves are challenged. The void's main tool to achieve all of this is simple: pain in the form of a near-constant depressive state that ebbs and flows. At its peak, your head feels like it is weighed down by a heavy invisible hand, as if you are being forced to look deep within your soul.

Despite how horrendous it seems, this experience is actually an opportunity of a lifetime. Carol Orsborn eloquently writes, "However you refer to it, one experiences it as the period that comes between what was and what's next. Within its darkness, it has no boundaries and no landmarks. When you are inside it, it feels like there will be no end. Fortunately, there are many 'survivors' who have journeyed through the void and emerged more vital, and more integrated, more connected to life's possibilities, not despite of, but because of the experience. The void is, after all, perhaps the most effective place of reordering of one's cognitive processes to take place, for that is where one is least invested in the structure that once circumscribed meaning in one's life."

In the beginning, this place was so dark that I could not even see my own self. We all intuitively know that in the midst of darkness, only light can save us, and so I began searching within my soul for torches to set alight. After years of searching, I found ten torches whose collective light could pierce through even the darkest core of the void. These torches exist within you, as well; all you have to do is find them.

1. The Torch of Surrender: The void is like a physician who is attempting to save our lives. Our unwillingness to cooperate with him could lead to death or serious harm. We have to peacefully surrender to the process rather than try to fight it or escape it.

2. The Torch of Painful Embrace: We naturally guard against physical and emotional pain. Yet emotional pain is somehow regarded as taboo; we are often ashamed of displaying it because we've been taught to see it as a sign of failure and personal weakness. Since pain is unavoidable in life, this attitude only makes it worse by adding layers of guilt, shame, and frustration. Ironically, pain is actually a well-meaning, misunderstood friend that we must embrace if we ever hope to heal. Pain is sometimes a warner who is standing at the frontlines of a looming disaster, yelling at the top of her voice, hoping that we heed the alarm and change the course of our lives. At other times, pain is simply inviting us to heal from old open wounds that are buried beneath the sands of time.

3. The Torch of Divine Friendship: The darkness of the void is overwhelming. We simply cannot face it by ourselves. The only being who can give us company in its loneliness is our Maker. Most of us don't realize that we are worthy enough to speak directly to the Divine without the need for intermediaries and saints. The prayers of a sincere heart can echo beyond the limits of the universe itself. Unfortunately, many people are unable to have this spiritual connection because "God" is simply a projection of their egos. Being vainly self-righteous and following our self-serving desires at the expense of doing what is right is a sign of this disease.

In the Qur'an, God is sometimes referred to as the "The Ever-Subtle One." So, as you embark on building this relationship, do not expect a grand vision or a thundering voice, but rather learn the subtle art of reading between the lines. Rabi'a, the 8th-century female mystic, used to pray:

"O God,
Whenever I listen to the voice of anything you have made
The rustling of the trees,
The trickling of water,
The cries of birds,
The flickering of shadow,
The roar of the wind,
The song of the thunder,
I hear it saying:
God is One!
Nothing can be compared with God!"

For you, for me, and for us all, I urge you to listen to the subtle whispers of God all around you. Like Rumi once said, "The language of God is silence."

Gather around,
in two's, three's, and four's,
at sundown,
on the last day of fall.
Gather around,
and hold each other's hearts.
There is but *one* yearning.
Gather around,
and listen to the sad song of life.
Gather around,
and hear the silent flute of destiny.
Gather around,
in two's, three's, and four's,
and listen...
Can you hear the whisper of the One?

4. **The Torch of Truth**: We enter the void as impostors, but only our true selves can emerge. For many of us, our true selves are buried alive beneath a mountain of lies and broken promises. They are suffocating, gasping for the air

of truth, trying to dig their way out from beneath the dirt of deceit. They weep, wail, and call out to no avail. Every time an opening is made revealing the rays of truth, a lie snuffs it out. Therefore, no more lies, manipulations, broken promises, unfulfilled commitments, two-faced deceit, and false claims of love.

Be truthful with your Maker, with yourself, and with everyone else. Only then will you *find* yourself; only then will you be able to see the path ahead with crystal clarity. And only then will you be able to distinguish right from wrong. When we utter a lie, it is our own spiritual vision that we damage.

Emerson once wrote, "Any attempt to make a good impression or a favourable appearance will instantly vitiate (spoil) the effect. But speak the truth, and all things alive or brute are vouchers, and the very roots of the grass underground there do seem to stir and move to bear witness."

5. The Torch of Hope: This is the central torch. Its light is the most illuminating when there is absolutely no hint of light anywhere else. You must never give up the hope that beyond the seemingly infinite ocean of hardship, the land of relief awaits.

I remain hopeful,
even when I *see* no reason to be.
The walls are high as heaven.
The doors are sealed shut.
Darkness envelopes me in layers.
Yet the sapling of hope is in my right,
and I dare to plant it,
knowing the world might end tonight.

6. The Torch of Humility: Humility means having a modest view of our importance. Our ego is the dragon that keeps us locked up in the prison of our self-centeredness. *An indication of our progress in lighting this torch is how often we place the needs of others over our own.*

7. The Torch of Integrity: In the void, many situations will test your character, pitting your personal desires directly against what is right. Every time you make the right choice, you will move forward, while every time you choose wrongly, you will be violently tossed many miles backwards. Hidden motives and self-serving actions are the vipers that lurk in the darkness of the void. The previously mentioned fourth Torch of Truth can help expose them.

8. The Torch of Meaning: There comes a point in many people's lives when they realize that what makes life rich and meaningful is being strongly connected to everyone from their Maker to their neighbour. The Prophet Jesus (peace be upon him) summed it all up when he said: *"The Lord our God, the Lord is one. Love the Lord your God with all your heart and with all your soul and with all your mind and with all your strength. And love your neighbor as yourself. There is no commandment greater than these."*

9. The Torch of Myth: The most important story is the story we tell ourselves about ourselves. Our lives came to a grounding halt because our story could no longer sail us forward. Yet we fearfully cling to it, like passengers refusing to jump off a sinking ship. The truth is that there is nothing to fear. We may still hold on to parts of our story that continue to be valuable. We can still honour the story that we wrote as children, for despite its dysfunctional elements, it was the best story we could tell to survive. However, now that we are beginning a new phase in our journey, we have to realize that only the adult storyteller within us is fit to be the narrator.

10. The Torch of Patience and Flow: The Prophet Muhammad (peace be upon him) said: "Victory is intertwined with patience, relief is intertwined with hardship, and with every difficulty there is ease."

If hope and divine love are what move us forward, then patience and flow are what save us from sliding backwards when faced with obstacles, setbacks, and provocations. To be patient is to hold ourselves back from acting out of frustration and instead choose to remain calm until the storm passes.

Flow, on the other hand, stems from the realization that our control over what happens to us is an illusion, and therefore, like a river, we gracefully flow over and around obstacles instead of allowing them to hold us back. Those who do not flow with the river of destiny are always stuck in the stagnant waters of frustration, anger, and resentment. They are like a hissing cat that is being dragged while its nails are dug deep into the ever-moving carpet of life.

Flow, Flow, Flow ...
Through every hardship and delight.
Flow, Flow, Flow ...
Through the darkness and the light.
Flow, Flow, Flow ...
Like a Monarch in its flight.
Flow, Flow, Flow ...
Like a river in the night.

This is the enriching and noble inner work that you will need to embark on. If it seems overwhelming, then remember that "a journey of a thousand miles always begins with one step." You are fully capable of completing this journey. Why else would you be called on to undertake it at this moment in your life?

Whether you realize it or not, you are a hero in the making. Joseph Campbell taught us that every hero that ever came before us, whether they were a noble prophet or a mythical adventurer, had to go through the phases of separation, initiation, and return.

In *separation*, they were physically or psychologically separated from their people.

In *initiation*, they were internally transformed by the knowledge, wisdom, and special powers they gained.

Finally, in *return*, they went back to their people and shared with them the gifts they were granted.

O Night of my soul, ever so dark!
Into your darkest corners, I shall embark.
Swimming through the deepest oceans of tears
Withstanding the howling winds of my fears
Seeking what every noble soul has sought
A treasure that is neither sold nor bought!

SELFHOOD

THE BOY INSIDE

He whipped his soul,
his entire life,
for what was not his fault.
And now the scars,
from all the wounds,
were there for all to see.
I saw the boy,
I saw the whip,
I saw through all the pain.
I told the man,
he was the boy,
and he was not to blame.
The man's tears fell,
he dropped the whip,
and hugged the little boy.
His burdens fell,
his wounds were healed,
and now he tasted joy.

*Illustrated by my friend and
fellow prisoner, Raheem.*

THE SHOES

My feet are bloodied and bruised,
from all my earthly travels.
Thorns of rejection and jagged rocks of disapproval,
are strewn and scattered everywhere.
For all my life,
I've tried,
without success,
to pave the earth with leather.
But now I walk in peace,
without any fear,
for I've put on my shoes of self-acceptance.

BIOHAZARD

There are dangerous men... *and then*... there are dangerous men. Howie belonged to the latter. He was a 60-year-old Indonesian friend of mine who lived on my prison block: short, bold, wore thick-rimmed glasses that made his eyes appear double their size, and always walked around with a permanent smile. As dangerous as he was, I never saw him get angry.

I believe Howie suffered from an early onset of Alzheimer's; I say this because whenever his door opened for *work*, he would come out with a towel, wondering aloud whether it was *shower time*. And whenever his door opened for *shower time*, he would come out wearing his white apron, wondering whether it was time for *work*. There is nothing funny about Alzheimer's, and yet Howie's jovial personality always turned this sad, reoccurring scene into a comic act.

I would not be exaggerating if I told you that half of my interactions with Howie occurred while he was on his toilet. "Are you enriching Uranium again, Howie?" I usually teased him as I passed by.

"Yes. I am developing a Weapon of Ass Destruction!" he would respond with his hilarious and equally cute accent.

Another thing about Howie was his obsession with television. Even when he was busy producing his lethal concoctions on his throne, he would move his TV to the edge of his bed so he wouldn't miss a second of his favourite drama, movie, or game show. (Howie loved watching everything, even hour-long infomercials.)

One day, his toilet broke down, so he came to me while I was speaking to my sister on the phone and asked if he could use my toilet.

"Of course, go right ahead," I said to him, not realizing the series of catastrophic events that this act of common decency would unleash. After a few minutes, two guards showed up to lock us up for the last count of the night. I said goodbye to my sister and made my way back to my cell, which was at the end of the block.

As I got closer, I saw Howie scurrying out of it with his pants still unbuttoned. "Thank you very much," he shouted as he ran past me to his cell, which was all the way at the front.

"No problem, Howie."
"HURRY UP, AMARA!" the guards yelled. So, I began sprinting towards my cell, and as soon as I entered it, everything went black.

I have no memory of what happened, so I can only assume that I was knocked out by the stench of whatever Howie unloaded in my toilet. It was an instant T.K.O.

"Wake up!"

"Are you there?"

My eyes slowly began to open. My vision was blurry. Everything was white. The walls were white, the lights were white, and two white shapes were standing over me as I lay on a medical bed. I struggled to make out what I was seeing, but as my senses slowly returned, I realized that the two white shapes were two men dressed in the type of suits you usually see at a chemical spill site. I think they're called biohazard suits.

"Mr. Amara," one of them said.

"Yes. What happened? Where am I?" I asked, feeling like I just survived a train accident.

"We are members of the International Atomic Energy Agency. At 22 hundred hours last night, a radiation signature usually associated with a nuclear weapon of mass destruction showed up on our global tracking device; the exact location was your prison cell. All the inmates living near your cell, including the two guards who were found unconscious in front of it, were hospitalized."

"We couldn't find the nuclear device; however, we did find radioactive residue on your toilet. Where did you hide the device, Mr. Amara?"

You can imagine how bizarre and confusing all this sounded to me;
I was speechless.

"Mr. Amara. You see that door to your left?" he said as he pointed towards it.

I turned and looked.

"Behind that door are three CSIS agents who would love nothing more than
to fly you to a black site location and do with you as they please. We're the good
guys here. It's in your best interest to cooperate with us."

"Honestly, I don't know what to tell you. I let an old man use my toilet, and
now I'm here."

They looked at each other, and then the taller one, who had been silent the
entire time, turned back to me and said, "Have it your way, Mr. Amara," as he
injected my arm with a needle, and I lost consciousness again.

....

....

....

When I woke up, I found myself lying on the ground in a windowless, door-
less room shaped like a perfect cube. It was completely empty; it had no bed, no
desk, and no toilet. As I slowly got up, I noticed that the entire room, from floor
to ceiling, was made up of hundreds of frowning faces of men and women, who
seemed to be directing their disapproving glances at me.

And then came the whispers...
"*You* are an *awful* human being."
        "*You* are an *awful* human being."

Having been around many schizophrenic inmates over the years, I felt
a panic set in, as I feared that I might be losing my mind—the last standing
fortress that stands between a man and the tormenting demons that imprison-
ment unleashes.

"I must be going crazy," I thought to myself, as I covered my eyes and began to feel sorry for myself.

"You are an *awful* human being," the whispers continued.

I started to cry and fell to the floor in a fetal position. As I sobbed, I felt a sharp longing for my mother and began to call out her name, hoping that by doing so, I could save the image of her beautiful face from fading away with the rest of my memories.

"You are an *awful* human being."

"STOP!" I shouted back as I covered my ears.

Suddenly, the whispers came to a screeching halt.

I stayed there on the ground, still curled up and still covering my ears. I wasn't crying anymore. I was simply relieved that the whispers had stopped. Oddly, I was beginning to enjoy the silence. It's amazing what we find comfort in when our whole world is going to hell.

After a while, I decided to get up, and as soon as I uncovered my ears...

"You are an *awful* human being," echoed once more.

I grimaced in pain and quickly covered my ears again. The whispers went silent immediately. This made me feel curious; so, I quickly alternated between uncovering and covering my ears, which resulted in the whispers turning on and off, as if I were turning a radio dial from side to side.

My eyes opened wide as I realized that I was not having a schizophrenic episode and that the whispers were real. A great relief washed over me like a friendly tide. The realization that I had not lost my mind uplifted my spirits in unimaginable ways.

A healthy mind is a blessing that most of us seldom appreciate.

I got up and began inspecting the cell with fresh eyes, immediately noticing tiny speakers built into the top corners of the room. I also noticed that all the walls, including the floor and ceiling, were actually large monitors that were protected by Plexiglas. It was all an illusion; the entire setup of the cell was intended to dehumanize and demoralize its occupants.

I can't recall how long I spent in that room. All I can remember is the countless battles that I waged against its never-ending attempts to destroy my sense of worth as a human being. On some days, I retreated, and on others, I advanced. But there was one particular day when I realized that I did not have to engage in this fight anymore, that if someone could not see my humanity, then perhaps it was *their* vision, and not mine, that needed to change.

The battle was over. I fell to my knees out of exhaustion and relief, and at that moment, I was inspired with words that caused the entire room to shatter before my eyes like glass...

The dragon has been slain.
My head is bowed,
and on my knees I stand.
The colour of my tears is red,
I see the break of dawn.
My heart weeps for what it lost,
yet my soul is full of joy.
For all the wisdom that it gained,
for all the lessons learned.

THE BORDERLINE

Sitting on the razor-thin borderline
of my worth
and lack thereof
cuts through me,
rendering each half of me
a citizen
of two neighbouring nations
perpetually at war.

A history of schizophrenic proportions.
Mixed messages of worth
and lack thereof
hurled back and forth
across this lonely border
leave me questioning:
Who am I?

Inherent dignity eludes me
like a swift gazelle
whose very traces
vanish with every leap.
A holy grail of sorts,
heard of, but never witnessed.

What makes one worthy?
Conditioned to feel so,
most people never ask.
But I am without a choice,
detained on this border
I can never leave
unless I find the answer.
And so, I pace frantically
as my mind digs through
the archives of a past
filled with torn pages
stained by undeserved indignities.

The past contains the roots
but not the branches.
So,
bewildered,
I dive towards the center of my heart,
towards the core of cores,
towards the seat of my intentions.

YOU

Believe me.
You are not your thoughts
that ramble on inside your head.

Nor your feelings and emotions
that drown you like a stormy sea.

Nor your God-given face,
be it handsome like the moon,
or plain as an empty page.

But who you are, my friend,
are your intentions;
your manners and your gestures,
the goodwill that you emanate
like the brightest sun that rose,
or the evil that you spread,
like the darkest night on earth.

WHAT IF?

What if each day was a test?
What if each day was a chance?
What if you lived to be a hundred years old?
That's three hundred and sixty-five thousand chances
to count how many hearts you shattered,
and how many hearts you pieced together again,
to tally how many times you sided
with your demons against your better angels
and how many times you took the road less travelled.

What if each day was a test?
What if each day was a chance?
To prove to us all...
Who you really, *really* are.

THE EGO'S SURPRISE

Surprise, surprise...
So, I'm not the only one.
There are others,
billions,
before me,
around me,
and many more to come.
With hopes,
and needs,
and dreams,
Surprise, surprise...
So, I'm just an atom in motion,
just a drop in the ocean,
just a sound in the commotion,
just a part of the land,
just a grain in the sand,
just a soul in God's hand,
Surprise, surprise...

FORGET YOURSELF

Forget yourself,
if only for a moment,
and see your worries slip away,
like a melting wall of ice.
Have no fear,
the world will still be here,
and so will you...

∞

Eckhart Tolle usually loses me after the first forty pages, but he nailed it when he wrote:

"Not to be able to stop thinking is a dreadful affliction, but we don't realize this because almost everybody else is suffering from it, so it is considered normal. This incessant mental noise prevents you from that realm of inner stillness that is inseparable from being. It also creates a false mind-made self that casts a shadow of fear and suffering. The philosopher Descartes believed he had found the most fundamental truth when he made his famous statement: "I think, therefore I am." He had, in fact, given expression to the most basic error: to equate thinking with Being and identity with thinking. The compulsive thinker, which means almost everyone, lives in a state of apparent separateness, in an insanely complex world of continuous problems and conflict, a world that reflects the ever-increasing fragmentation of the mind...Identification with your mind creates an opaque screen of concepts, labels, images, words, judgments, and definitions that blocks all true relationships. It comes between you and yourself; between you and your fellow man and woman; between you and nature; between you and God."

VULNERABLE

Yes,
I choose to be vulnerable,
eleven times,
out of ten.
To give myself to you,
so you could,
if you choose,
trample me beneath your feet.

It's not easy living that way,
but it's as deep as the ocean,
and as profound as the sunrise,
and as beautiful as a nightingale,
ascending on a starry summer night.

Yes,
I choose to be vulnerable,
because you can't truly love someone,
or raise a child,
or be touched by God,
without it.

THEY SAY, I SAY, YOU SAY...

The past,
   The present,
      The future.
"Live in the present," they say.
But how can that be?
When the past haunts us like a ghost,
and the future looms over us with its menacing shadow.
"There is no before," the madman said,
as he tried to escape his past.
"And there is no after," the madwoman said,
as she tried to ignore her future.
Yet the past, the present, and the future are the most intimate of friends,
the trinity of trinities.

So here is what I say:
But who am I to say anything?
Regardless, I say,
I say, even if only to hear myself,
   I say, because I can,
      I say, because I will,
I say this:
"The past is a friend waiting to be accepted.
The present is a wrestler waiting to be challenged.
And the future is a dream waiting to be dreamed."
There! I said it,
So what will you say?

Triumph

I feel my soul surging,
like a tidal wave,
like a giant running forth,
like a ferocious wind,
like a wild stallion freed,
earth below me trembling,
ropes creaking from the tension,
walls retreating in defeat.
There is no anger here,
No resentment,
No conceit.

THE EAGLE'S FLIGHT

Oh, how my spirit soars!
Above this place of tears and gloom,
resurrected after dying,
from the ashes of my doom.
Like an eagle in full flight,
released, unleashed,
shackles broken, decimated, left behind
forever.
Never ever to be locked again,
delivered from despair's deepest pit,
bearing words of hope and wisdom that I spit,
into dying hearts of people down below,
in the darkest, coldest, saddest places that I know.
Oh, how my spirit soars!
Above this place of tears and gloom,
resurrected after dying,
from the ashes of my doom.

PART

7

JOY

THE NIHILIST

It was Saturday night, and that could only mean one thing: camel racing!

I was reclining on my bed, waiting for the race to begin on ESPN Desert Sports, while my friend, Sami, stood next to me.

Prison cells are tiny by design. Imagine a steel bed, a steel desk, a TV stand, a steel toilet, and a steel sink, all crammed in a room just a little bigger than your walk-in closet.

Then add two people.

The most popular camel race announcer on the planet, "Lightning Larabie," appeared on screen as the crowd in the stands began to cheer his name. He once claimed that one of his ancestors was half man, half camel. Everyone believed him. However, official documents later surfaced revealing that he was just a French farm boy from Quebec.

"Ladies and gents, it looks like the moment of truth is upon us…"

DING! DING! DING! DING! DING! DING! DING! DING!

Oh, and the race begins!
Donaldhump gets the jump
Then *Whatsmells*
Smoothsand is close in third
They're making the turn
Donaldhump keeps the lead.
Oh, *Whatsmells* is making his move!
Just look at those humps!
Smoothsand is falling behind.
Whatsmells is neck and neck with *Donaldhump*
It's a close race
Look at that sand fly!
Holy camel hoof!

Whatsmells pushes ahead
Oh my goodness! He's taken the lead.
He's going! going! GONE!
UNBELIEVABLE! UNBELIEVABLE!
HISTORY HAS JUST BEEN MADE!
WHATSMELLS HAS JUST WON THE SAHARA DERBY
TO CAPTURE THE TRIPLE
HUMP FOR THE FIRST TIME EVER!
THE CROWD IS GOING WILD IN THE SAND!
IT'S PANDEMONIUM!
Oh, uh! The A.Ks are coming out!
I'm taking cover
TA! TA! TA! TATATAT! TATTAT!

SIGNAL LOST-STATIC/////////// SIGNAL LOST-STATIC/////////// SIGNAL LOST

Meanwhile, I was losing my mind, jumping on my bed, yelling at the top of
my lungs, shooting my imaginary pistol *directly* upwards (like a typical Arab, so
the bullets could come back down and hit me)—and following it all up with the
most ridiculous cultural dance I could pull off.

I couldn't believe what I just witnessed! I've been watching camel racing
since I was just 26 *days* old, and it never crossed my mind that I would ever
live to see this moment!

My friend, Sami, on the other hand, just stood there like a statue, staring
despondently at the screen without a trace of emotion. He'd been depressed like
this ever since I met him. I tried putting him on antidepressants, but his condi-
tion didn't improve; by the way, Sami was a donkey.

"Sami, man, cheer up! It's not that bad. Sure, we're in prison, but things can
always be worse."

"My name is not Sami," he somberly said in a deep, baritone voice as he spoke for the first time. Having been used to his silence, it took me a few seconds to process his words.

"So, what's your name then?"

"My name is Friedrich Nietzsche."

"That's the name of a famous German philosopher!"

"Yes. My father admired him greatly, so he named me after him. I personally prefer Nihilist philosophers."

"I had no idea that donkeys were into philosophy, but like I said, you can't just be depressed all the time. I mean, I get it; it happens to all of us, but you have to find a way to come out of it. You can't just surrender to it."

I was becoming used to his delayed responses by now. He appeared to be pondering.

"What is the point of being alive?" he suddenly started to speak again. "Suffering stamps us with its ugly mark from the moment we are born. Do we not enter this world crying? As children, our innocence is stripped away; as youth, our idealism is smashed to bits; and as adults, we're forced to bury our dreams in the cemetery of our future graves. Innocence lost, ideals abandoned, and the curse of living while one's dreams are dead. Everything we know will disappear, and everyone we love will die. Meaningless... It's all meaningless."

I was still standing on my bed when he spoke those words. So, I slowly stepped down and sat on its edge, like a boy dangling his feet down a well. I sat there for a moment with my head bowed, silently taking in the full weight of his words, with all their truth, pain, and sadness.

"I get what you mean," I began to answer. "Everything you said makes sense, but only when you view life through a selfish lens. The truth is that life is not just about you; *in fact, it never was*. Countless other beings share this world with you. A man could suffer much in life, yet still go on to relieve someone else of their suffering. He could have no reason to smile or laugh for years, yet still go on to be the reason for someone else's joy and laughter. You're right; life will always be meaningless...*until we learn to look beyond ourselves*."

I noticed the expression on his face began to dissipate.

"What you said...." he began slowly, "was profound..."

An awkward silence followed—the kind we experience after having a deep exchange with someone else...

Trying to break the ice, he said, "Umm....*Whatsmells*.... *Whatsmells* was magnificent tonight."

So, I smiled and answered, "Yes....yes he was, wasn't he? So, what do you want to watch tonight?"

"I love *Animal Cops: Philadelphia*," he responded.

"Alright," I said with a chuckle. "*Animal Cops* it'll be."

We spent the rest of the night watching TV, joking around, talking about our previous lives, and eating stale Uncle Ray's Hot Chips. It was fantastic!

OFFICER ROBINSON'S REPORT

"At the 10:30 night count, Mr. Amara and his donkey were observed braying back and forth. Their conversation was completely meaningless. I recommend that Mr. Amara be transferred to the Regional Treatment Center for a psychiatric evaluation."

Warden's Comment:
Recommendation approved

How was your day?

How was your day?
Was it one to remember?
Or one to forget?
Was it harsh like a torturer's heart?
Or a beautiful work of art?
Did it make you wish it was your last?
Or like a breeze, it blew by fast?
Perhaps it was between all that.
Indeed, most days are just like that!

The Girl with the Tattered Crimson Dress

We could escape from prison, but we can never escape from ourselves. We could try to distract ourselves from our own beings by flooding our lives with every luxury our hearts desire. We could try to fulfill every fantasy our minds can conjure. We could do all this and may even feel "happy" for a while, but soon, that hollow feeling, that sharp, painful angst, returns.

Almost everything we do in life, we do to feel "happy," yet most of us, including myself, have never taken a moment to ponder over what this seemingly simple word actually means.

My search for the meaning of "happiness" began in a mundane fashion at the prison library. I picked up books like *Stumbling Upon Happiness*, *Happier*, *The Happiness Project*, and *The Happiness Equation*. These were just the titles available. Apparently, many other books have been written on the subject, such as *The Art of Happiness*, *The Conquest of Happiness*, *The Psychology of Happiness*, *The How of Happiness*, and so on.

In one of the books, I found a reference to a psychological study that cited 15 different academic definitions of happiness! People have been so fascinated by this topic that scholars as ancient as Aristotle have written on it.

Not being one to be satisfied by mere reading, I hosted a mini-conference in the prison yard with three learned cons. As I walked away dissatisfied with their answers, a short Indonesian man with balding gray hair, thick glasses, and a big semi-permanent smile greeted me and shook my hand. I immediately asked him about his opinion on happiness, and he answered me with an even wider grin: "Happiness is happiness!"

Technically, he was right, or rather, he was not wrong. No one can deny that a soccer ball is a soccer ball... but that's not a real answer, is it? Disqualification was the Indonesian man's fate, and the search continued.

In *Happier*, Tal Ben-Shahar's equation for happiness is, "Meaningful life + present pleasure = happiness."

He writes: "We need the experience of meaning and the experience of positive emotions; we need the present and future benefit. My theory of happiness draws on the works of Freud as well as Frankl. Freud's pleasure principle says that we are fundamentally driven by the instinctual need for pleasure. Frankl argues that we are motivated by a will to meaning rather than by a will to pleasure – he says, 'Striving for meaning in one's life is the primary motivational force in man.' In the context of finding happiness, there is some truth in both Freud's and Frankl's theories. We need to gratify both the will for pleasure and the will for meaning if we are to lead a fulfilling, happy life."

I was temporarily convinced by this until he mentioned that people in difficult circumstances, due to the absence of pleasure, could NOT be happy. (Hold this thought in your right pocket for a moment because I will return to it.) When I read this, I thought, *If such people could not be happy, then what could they be?*

Beautiful.

There is something incredibly beautiful about a human being who strives to be as positive and good as they can be despite the harshness of their lives. Though their backs are on the verge of collapse from all the burdens they have to carry, they somehow find the strength to hold on to their values and dignity. Such people never blame their Creator for their misfortunes; but surprisingly, they thank Him. They never backstab those around them; instead, they heal and uplift them. A person who chooses to behave in this manner exemplifies the pinnacle of human beauty in such circumstances.

Omar bin Al Khattab once said: "The best moments of our lives were those lived in patience." Sigmund Freud echoed his sentiment 1300 years later when he wrote, "One day, in retrospect, the years of struggle will strike you as the most beautiful."

So, people living in hardship could achieve beauty, but I still wondered whether Ben-Shahar was right about happiness being beyond their reach. This question nagged at me for some time until I remembered the words of ex-Soviet prison camp survivor Aleksandr Solzhenitsyn, who wrote:

"If a miracle happens (in prison) and I get a quiet Sunday off, and in the course of the day my soul thaws out and is at ease, there may not have been any change for the better in my objective situation, but the prison yoke lies more lightly on me. And then suppose, I have a really satisfying conversation or read an honest page –

there I am, on the crest of a wave! I've had no real life for many years, but I forget it! I'm weightless, I'm suspended in space, I am disembodied. I lie there on top of my bunk, I look at the ceiling just above me — it's bare, the plaster's peeling — but I shudder with the sheer bliss of being! I fall asleep on the wings of happiness! No president or prime minister can go to sleep as content with the Sunday behind him." And that's when it hit me.

Everyone wants to be happy,
yet no one knows what it means.
I asked one hundred wise men,
One thousand answers I received.
With absolute disappointment,
Empty-handed I returned.
On a path through a dark forest,
a little girl passed me by.
With hair as dark as charcoal,
and a tattered crimson dress.
Wearing dirt upon her cheeks,
walking softly upon bare feet.
Her face was full of innocence,
and her smile was a source of light.
As she vanished in the distance,
I heard the echo of her song:

"Most people wish to be happy,
yet in darkness, they choose to hide.
Happiness is a blessing,
that rises like the Sun.
If the skies are clear and blue,
and the night has come and gone.
And you happen to be out there somewhere
with a heart that's open wide.
Then you shall have your share of it,
and you'll feel it deep inside.
Happiness is like a little girl,
in a tattered crimson dress.
You won't know she's passing by,
if you're trapped inside a mess!"

Poetic Genes

My father?
My father is an enigma.
A puzzle I have yet to solve.

I still remember his song (or prayer):
   "O Zakaria, O Zakaria!
   May you fall into a pit of poop
   And find no one to pull you out of it!"
Prophetic words that make me smile to this day.
Oh! and by the way,
Now I know where my poetry flows from.
I love you, Baba!

WORTHLESS

Our sense of worthlessness is always built on an exaggerated story we tell ourselves. Humour can help us see it.

I'm from a town called Worthless.
East of Shame and North of Guilt.
Population: Unknown (They felt unworthy of being counted).
Popular dish: Roasted Self-esteem with Meek salad.
Favourite pastime: Practicing invisibility.
Hometown hero: Yours truly.

LEITA'S CABIN

What on earth am I doing here? I ask myself as I stand at the front steps of a quiet cabin in the Yukon while the sun majestically begins to rise behind me, unveiling a desert made of snow.

What on earth am I doing here? I ask again, even though I know the answer.

Chasing after a phantom named Leita...

I knock on the door, knowing that no one will answer.

We know many things before we know them...

I push the door and slowly walk inside.

The place is gently warm.

I look around...

Simple but elegant furniture.

Kitchen cupboards stuffed with ingredients from every culture.

Cat fur everywhere.

Half-melted candles.

And as I reach the end of my panoramic examination, a giant portrait on the back wall captures my attention and stills me into hypnotic surrender.

The sunlight is now flooding the cabin, and the portrait's golden frame shines and shimmers.

It is of two elderly figures standing side by side. The affection between them has a near-cosmic effect that radiates outwards and gently lands on the perceiving hearts of onlookers.

I felt it too, now.

This was her core...

The smile behind her smile,
and the gentle but fierce kindness that knew no *bounds*...

Funny that I should use *that* word. I remember her telling me once that she wanted to experiment with mushrooms to learn how to set personal *boundaries*.

But now, as I stood mesmerized by the beauty of this portrait, I realized just how impossible her task must have been. Just imagine a little girl trying to contain the rays of the sun with the palms of her hands.

Heh, mushrooms!
I laughed to myself as I headed towards the door,
knowing now what I had always known...

GIUSEPPE

I was lying in my bed, sipping on cold milk and eating raisins. My friend, Giuseppe, a balding red rooster with just one eye, stood on a stool beside my bed, eating sunflower seeds and spitting the shells out on the floor like the inconsiderate sleazeball that he was. Giuseppe was quite a character, an Italian immigrant who managed to graduate from both Harvard's and MIT's schools of business at the same time. He then went on to become a successful stockbroker on Wall Street until the 2008 financial crisis claimed him as one of its victims. Since roosters have no moral misgivings, Giuseppe simply jumped over to the dark side and began using pyramid schemes to finance his extravagant lifestyle.

Everything was going well for Giuseppe until one day, his wife found feathers that belonged to another hen in one of his coats. Instantly, his wife went ballistic. In a fit of blinding Italian fury, she ran over to his emperor-size bed as he was taking his afternoon siesta and pecked the living daylights out of him.

A struggle then ensued between them as the now one-eyed Giuseppe was fighting for his life. The neighbours overheard the commotion and called the police. The two stopped fighting when the cops arrived, and Giuseppe's wife claimed self-defence. With one eye missing and half of his feathers gone, the evidence was pointing in her direction. But since Giuseppe had a natural sleazeball look about him, it only took one quick glance to declare him guilty and charge him with domestic abuse.

Giuseppe's troubles didn't end there; his wife went on to spill the beans on his fraudulent enterprise, which led to further charges. In the end, Giuseppe received 10 years for all his troubles, and that's how he ended up in a prison cell, with nothing to do but stand on a stool and ponder over how it all went so south.

Still lying in my bed with nothing to watch on TV, I looked at my clear plastic cup that was nearly empty and began swooshing it like a wine connoisseur. As I stared at the remaining milk that was swirling around and around at the bottom of the cup, I suddenly felt the type of inspiration that poets feel before writing an epic poem.

"Giuseppe," I began asking, barely containing my enthusiasm, "do you think there is a market for camel milk in Canada?"

He bobbed his little head upwards and turned towards me with his one good eye. Giuseppe always paused for a second or two before speaking. This delay gave whatever he was about to say an air of authority, even if it was complete rubbish.

"Sonny," he said, sounding like Al Pacino, "With the right sales pitch, you could sell camel shit!"

Conciseness is the hallmark of wise speech.

"Hmmm..." I muttered as I began to doze off.

When I opened my eyes again, I saw that I was on a set of some sort, dressed in a sparkling white robe and a majestic headset similar to the one worn by Lawrence of Arabia. When I looked to my immediate right, I saw a camel standing beside me. *I must be dreaming*, I thought.

"Welcome to Dragon's Den!"

I looked ahead and saw three men and one woman sitting in chairs, all beaming with anticipation.

"What's your name?" the kind-looking red-headed lady asked me.

Before I could gather my thoughts, I answered her as if possessed by someone else—a more confident, chauvinistic version of myself.

"My name is *Zakaria Amara*.... the greatest camel herder of *all time*."

The camel beside me nodded in agreement.

"So, what do you have for us today?" the mean-looking bald man asked.

"CaMooo! The finest camel milk in the world!"

They all burst into laughter; one of them even fell on all fours and began slapping the ground hysterically.

"You gotta be kidding me. YOU came on this show to sell CAMEL MILK?!" the mean one exclaimed.

The real me would have melted away like a candle, but to my surprise, I began to speak with supreme confidence and authority.

"CaMooo is not just a delicious beverage; it's also a revolutionary health product proven to cure cancer, diabetes, Alzheimer's, Parkinson's, depression, itchy feet, high blood pressure, low blood pressure, ADD, DVD, an angry wife, and the Bubonic plague."

I was running out of illnesses, so I decided to go for the home run...

"And if you drink one gallon a day, then you will live forever!" I said dramatically.

Their facial expressions went from mocking to dazzled, and like excited children, they all asked at once, "DO YOU HAVE A SAMPLE WE CAN TRY?"

"Of course!" I said with a victorious smile.

I had a large plastic container, so I simply squatted under the camel and began milking it on live television. When the container was finally filled, I walked over to the red-headed lady who was sitting on the far right, knelt before her, and offered her the milk as if it were the most precious jewel on Earth.

"Mmmm... It's delicious!" she commented as she looked over to her colleagues with approval. "I would love to try this with my cereal!"

She then passed the container over to her right, and the audience heard comments like, "Camel milk! Where have you been all my life?" "It reminds me of my mother's milk," and "Can I keep this sample?"

Feeling like a great ancient conqueror, I proudly strutted back to the center of the set...

clink clink clink clink DUFF!

I suddenly awoke to the sound of my door opening. My alarm clock indicated that it was 7:30 a.m. I looked at the floor and noticed it was covered by a three-inch carpet made of sunflower seed shells. Giuseppe was on my toilet, drinking from its refreshing water.

"You know something, Giuseppe..." I began to say. "You're an absolute genius! Thank you!"

He looked up with toilet water still dripping from his beak, turned towards me with his one good eye, and said, "Hey! Fuggedaboutit! Bada-bing-bada-boom!" as he jumped off the toilet like Super Mario and walked out the door.

MODERNITY

OPERATION CAMEL JOCKEY

"Colonel, we have positive identification of our target, but there is a problem, Sir," a drone operator spoke into his headset as he stared at his computer screen.

"What's the problem, Sargent?" the colonel's voice crackled through.

"Sir, the target appears to be riding a camel."

"A camel?!"

"Yes, Sir."

"They have camels in Canadian prisons? Are you sure about this, Sargent?"

"Yes, Sir; the target has been circling the empty prison yard on a camel for the last 30 minutes."

"Hmm..."

"Colonel?"

"Proceed with the strike, Sargent."

"But Sir, nothing in the WWBYWWFY protocols allows us to target animals; killing the camel might spark an international incident."

"Fair enough. Let me consult with the chain of command and get back to you. In the meantime, if the target separates himself from the camel, strike him immediately."

"Yes, Sir! Copy!"

The world looks so different when you're sitting on top of a camel, I thought as I meditatively swayed from side to side, staring into the distance, feeling utterly intoxicated by the sheer beauty of our universe.

I loved coming out at night and seeing my camel waiting for me. Once I mounted him, he would suddenly rise, and I would feel as if I were being catapulted up to the heavens, leaving behind all my worries and troubles, feeling the heavy yoke of prison slide off me. The experience was mystical.

His name was Hump... Donald Hump.

I got him a few months ago after winning a lawsuit against the government for illegally placing me in solitary confinement for years. I've always been a reasonable man, so when the judge ruled in my favour and asked me what I wanted for compensation, I stood, and without hesitation, asked for either a trillion dollars or a camel. *Reasonable men always provide options.*

The judge immediately applauded me for my reasonableness and turned towards the Crown for his response, but before he could fully turn, the Crown had already stood and almost tripped over his words as he quickly said: "We'll give him the camel, Your Honour! He can have the camel!"

Everyone was happy with this outcome, except, of course, for Corrections Canada, which had to airlift a camel from the deserts of Arabia and house it in a Maximum Security prison. In the days before Donald's arrival, I was so ecstatic that I could hardly sleep. (Even when I did catch a nap, all I dreamt about were camels.) Finally, one day, as I was pacing in my cell with anxious anticipation, I heard an all-too-familiar *clink clink clink clink DUFF!*

My cell door opened as I simultaneously heard these heavenly words announced over the P.A. system: "Mr. Amara. Head to the yard, please. Your camel is here. Your camel is here."

I quickly put on my clothes and practically ran to the yard.

When I first locked eyes with Donald, I felt an instant connection. I could sense that he felt relieved to see a fellow desert dweller. Standing beside Donald was a camel expert wearing a safari hat. He was there to teach me how to take care of him, but to both my surprise and his, I needed no training! Everything came to me naturally! The expert mused that I was genetically predisposed to handling camels and, with sincere sadness, said that I missed my calling in life.

At first, I wanted to call my camel Al Jamal Al Kabeer, "The Great Camel" but I feared that such a name would hamper his assimilation into Canadian society. I didn't want him to be one of those guys who always had to introduce himself by saying, "My name is Al Jamal Al Kabeer, but you can call me Al," so I just called him "Donald" instead. The "Hump" part came later, when I told my friend, Herb, what his name was, and he instantly blurted out, "Donald Hump!" When the other prisoners standing nearby heard this, they all began chanting, "Donald Hump! Donald Hump!"

Instantly, Donald became the center of attention, the number one reason why we went outside. In fact, some men who never used to come out before began doing so when Donald arrived. One thing that struck me was the instant calming effect that being with Donald had on them. They all seemed to turn into innocent children when he was around.

Donald had many skills and talents, the most surprising of which was his ability to run towards a football and kick it. Sometimes, he would kick it so far and high that it would go beyond the fence. Soon after discovering this talent, prisoners began to place bets on where the ball would land. This betting game usually started with the customary, "Donald Hump! Donald Hump!"

Which would soon be followed by,

"Kick *that* ball! Kick *that* ball!"

Upon hearing this, Donald's ears would perk up, and he would begin to strut with pride towards the center of the yard where the ball awaited him.

Whenever a new prisoner arrived, Donald had a funny habit of groaning with surprise upon seeing them; he would then quickly walk over to the nearest fence and look up at the razor wire, look back at me, and then look back up at the wire again. You see, in his mind, Donald thought the fence was there to **prevent** people from coming in, yet in they came each day. This absolutely baffled him!

Tonight was a good night.

It was time for me to pray, so I softly tapped Donald on his side, and he gracefully kneeled down as I dismounted him. While gently patting him on the head, I smiled as I watched him eat dates from my hand. I then walked over to a grassy patch and began to pray.

As I prostrated my face on the ground, I asked God to take care of my beautiful daughter and to forgive me for my shortcomings, especially the mess I left behind as a younger man.

The world can be a painful place to live in. It's only here, between the hands of my Maker, that I have ever felt most accepted, most loved. A serene feeling overcame me, and my tears began to flow, as did my buried pain. Suddenly, my vision was filled with light that enveloped everything. Time seemed to pause and move swiftly all at once: I saw flowers of all kinds bursting forth in slow and fast motion; blue, yellow, and crimson red...

8:20 P.M. – TOSA Headquarters, North Virginia

"Colonel, the target has been hit."

"Is that animal still alive?"

"Uh, are you referring to the camel, Sir?"

"Yes, Sargent."

"The camel is unharmed, Sir."

"Good work! Fly the drone back to home base and prepare for debriefing."

"Yes, Sir. Copy."

I CAN'T BREATHE

I wrote this poem shortly after the death of George Floyd.

∞

Both white and black are breathing,
the same colourless air.
Show me what's fair.
Does anyone care?
Wake me up from this nightmare!

Fires raging
on Earth,
and in hearts, blazing.
Foul and dark hatred.
I can't breathe!

I can't breathe this air no more.
the fish are dying in the seas,
and soon we'll have no more trees,
Or bees,
courtesy of man-made catastrophes.
I can't breathe!

Kicked out of our homes
by bank-robbing bankers.
No divine anchors.
This ship is sinking.
The air is stinking.
I can't breathe!

Nuclear arms,
Boots of war treading forth,
    Drone
        strikes,
Indiscriminately discriminate
Injustice that is permanent.
Are the last days finally eminent?
I can't breathe!

Mother!
Wake me up from this nightmare!
Hug me like you used to,
and promise that I'll be okay.
Oh! How I wait for the day when we all shall say,
Let us pray, let us pray.
let us pray for peace,
let us pray for love,
let us pray for air from up above.

GEORGE
PERRY
FLOYD JR.
(October 14, 1973
– May 25, 2020)

SUBLIMATION

Sublimation: Channeling one's needs and urges into productive and healthy actions.

Why are we so miserable?
Why am *I* so miserable?
Modernity teaches us
to obsessively watch over
the seeds of our discontent
and keep watering them,
until they grow
into towering shadows
whose dark shade we can never escape.
Our bodies may be well-groomed and fed,
but our souls are withering away,
like the dying leaves of September.
There is much to be happy about,
and much else to do,
besides this narcissistic watering.
Freud may have been wrong about many things,
but sublimation was not one of them.

THE ENDLESS FALL

Oh, how lonely we've become!
Marching through empty streets
to the beat of a selfish drum.
We've cut the ties that bind us all
to heaven, to kin, to a stranger's call,
and now we fall, and now we fall,
like dying leaves,
in an endless fall.

MODERN MAN

I lost my wings,
that I once had,
with which I used to fly.

Beyond the clouds,
beyond the stars,
beyond this earthly realm.

And now I live,
alone inside,
this empty, lonely loft.

I once was whole,
I'm shattered now,
I'm such a scattered mess!

My body is here,
my mind is there,
and my soul is somewhere else...

THE MAN DELUSION

This is the material world,
but beside it,
around it,
inside it,
here,
there,
and everywhere,
exists the immaterial.

"Where is *God?!*"
Dawkins asks.
As if he will find Him with a microscope,
or a telescope,
or a stethoscope,
or a sky-piercing tower, as Pharaoh once suggested.
But Rumi was right:
"When you look for God
look for Him in the look of your eyes
in the thought of looking, *near to yourself than yourself,*
or in things that have happened to you.
There's no need to go outside.
Be melting snow.
Wash yourself of yourself."

THE PROPHET DARWIN

I met a man who said to me,
can you believe that God could be?
With all the stories that fossils tell,
the tales you tell don't ring a bell.
The only prophet my faith is in
is an Englishman I call Darwin.

I said to him suppose that I,
believed that God was but a lie.
That our universe was born by chance,
and God's real name was Happenstance.
That my forefathers were great big apes,
stumbling around, searching for grapes.
That good and evil on our whims depend,
that death was the end that ends all ends.
That this life we live is meaningless,
with no real goal or great purpose.

Then, my dear friend, I ask you this:
When the winds of hardship begin to hiss,
and the nights of sorrow consume my cheers,
and my face is washed by streams of tears,
and my heart is broken like an old tree,
and relief's gatekeeper has tossed the key,
and I find myself alone in darkness,
with no one to speak to except my madness,
weak and broken without any power,
can Darwin help me in that hour?

DESPISED SUBJECT MATTER

Life.
It really is a mystery.
Sometimes we're happy,
sometimes we're sad.
Sometimes we're empty,
sometimes we're full.
But always seeking,
never satisfied.
Or is it just me?

The curse,
or the blessing,
of a curious mind;
wanting life to be so much more
than it seems.
I wonder,
what is behind the veil?
I am getting older,
grey signs keep on surprising me.

Whenever I stand before the mirror,
they whisper,
"It's only a matter of time..."
Modern people hate this kind of talk.
We hide our elders in retirement homes,
as to not be reminded
of the inevitable,
while we amuse ourselves to death.

But I stubbornly refuse to be
a sheep, blindly guided to the slaughter.
I want my eyes to be wide open,
when it happens...

ANGUISH

After his wife's battle with cancer, my brother began to frequent a nearby graveyard. I wrote this for him.

∞

I visit the graveyard
daily,
to try and feel
what you must be feeling,
all the time.

Death has stared you in the eyes,
and now,
every sight is tainted
by that encounter.

What does life mean?
when you now know
what it means to die.

I get it.
Death does turn every colour
into the saddest of grey.
But you're alive,
and the breath of God still resides within you.

You may have stepped halfway into the afterlife,
but your other half is *still* with us...

SURRENDER

Pillars of Peace

Peace...
To be content with God's ways,
yet be open to change.
To be still,
yet be ready to move.
To be unafraid,
yet be fear's neighbour.
To embrace yourself,
yet hunger for growth.
To leave room for others,
yet keep a small room for yourself.
Peace...

A Cure for Anxiety

Learn to hold your fear.
A thousand speared warriors are marching your way.
Do not run.
Do not hide.
Do not fight.
Just sit aside and let them pass.
If uncertainty breeds anxiety,
and if nothing in life is certain,
then why not just surrender your illusions of control?

A man scrambles on a beach
to hold the bad waves at bay,
and to keep the good waves coming.
Utterly frustrated and exhausted,
he finally sits down and surrenders:
Peace!
A persistent wound on a man's heel
once turned him into the best of archers.
In every scar, there is a gift, and in every gift, there is a curse.

THE PLACE BETWEEN

Looking for that place
    inside me,
where my fate
and my will
    meet,
without colliding.

Too many years wasted,
leaving to fate what should be willed
while trying to will what is not fated.

50,000 Years Before Existence

My fate
hangs around my neck
like a necklace.

My life is an outline of a portrait
drawn by God
that I must paint with my deeds.

Freewill and Fate
are like twin horses
that we ride standing,
not knowing which is which
until the race is over.
There can be no peace,
no rest,
and no stillness of the mind,
without embracing destiny.
Wholehearted surrender...

Glimpsing into the secrets of the universe,
"Maktoob," the Arabs said,
   "It is written."
            Your life,
                  and your death;
                        your sorrows,
                              and your joys;
                                    every grain of rice,
                                          and every golden coin,
on its way to you,
was marked with your name,
50,000 years before existence.

What hit you was never meant to miss you,
and what missed you was never meant to hit you.
The pens of destiny have been lifted,
and their ink has long dried.

SURRENDER

I didn't know it at the time, but this was the **last** poem I wrote before my release from prison.

∞

I finally learned to surrender,
entirely,
wholeheartedly,
without resistance.

Inner revolution.
White flags calmly swaying in the wind.
The heart, not mind, is king again.

Anxiety and despair,
shadow ministers of the mind,
exiled and banished,
to the outer limits of consciousness.

Nearly forgotten memories returning,
slowly,
like freed prisoners,
The children are free again!

Sublime surrender echoes
through every fibre of my being.

Thoughts are now like endless rows of soldiers,
all bowing,
in one direction.

Weapons down forever.
The time has come,
for everlasting peace...

The Unguarded Gates

For most, life is either an adventure that should be celebrated or a catastrophe that can't end soon enough.

When I awoke to my 5,475th morning in prison, I could definitely tell you that I belonged to the latter category.

Our cell doors had opened a few minutes ago, but I just couldn't muster the will or the motivation to get up and face another groundhog day. The monotony of this place is like a python that finds a way to squeeze your soul just a little tighter with every passing day.

I heard someone yelling something from afar but couldn't make out what they were saying. My mood was already in the toilet, and so, this only added to my irritation. Every federal inmate knows that silence rules the morning hours. Some of them had to learn this lesson the hard way.

"THE GUARDS ARE GONE!" someone yelled again, but from somewhere close by.

My irritation turned into curiosity as I immediately got off my bed, put on my institutional blue jeans, and left to find out what the morning commotion was all about.

Most of the convicts had already left my living block and were gathered downstairs around the central "bubble," where officers usually sat all day to monitor our tortured lives. A few inmates were already trying to unlock the bubble's door. I knew there were weapons in that room and had no interest in being around for the next scene, so I quickly walked away and took another set of stairs that led to the building's main door.

The prison compound contained four main units that faced each other with a courtyard in the middle. To my surprise, I found the door wide open, and as I stood at its edge, I looked outside and couldn't see a single guard or staff member in sight. I hesitated for a while as I debated whether I should step outside under these strange circumstances. I had never contemplated escape, and the last thing I wanted was to get shipped back to Maximum Security where I languished for 13 years. I am usually not impulsive, but my legs betrayed me at that moment, and I suddenly found myself in the courtyard, alone beneath the summer sky.

"Attention inside people," the loudspeakers suddenly blared. "Please proceed to the main gate. Your days of captivity are over."

I pinched myself to make sure that I was not dreaming.

"Attention inside people..." the announcement repeated itself again.

I remained standing there, wondering whether I had lost my mind—a fear that has haunted me ever since I found myself in the belly of this beast.

"This must be one of those lucid dreams," I assured myself as I began walking towards the long dirt path to the main gate.

The sky was blue with mercy, and the sun was bright with friendship. I couldn't describe to you what I was beginning to feel because I had never felt that way before.

As the main gate became visible in the distance, I noticed a single man standing there beside a black horse. His features revealed themselves to me with every passing step. He was aged and of Indigenous descent. He had long silver hair and wore traditional brown clothing, and although he held a spear in his hand, which he used to lean on, he stood with such dignity that emanated neither arrogance nor weakness.

When I finally reached him, he greeted me while still gazing ahead into the distance as if he were peering into the soul of the universe. Though his face was worn out by the passage of the years, his eyes still glittered like two bright, shimmering stars. He spoke slowly. He said that his name was Geronimo and instructed me to make my way to the small tent that stood just beyond the gate.

I thanked him and slowly walked in that direction. When I finally reached it, I awaited permission to enter.

"Tanisi," a female voice sounded from inside.

I slowly entered and spotted an elderly lady sitting cross-legged on the ground all by herself. She greeted me with a bright and comforting smile that instantly soothed the wounds left behind by all the unforgiving years in captivity.

I couldn't help myself. Tears began to roll down my face, and my hands began to tremble. She slowly got up and walked towards me as I continued to weep. She then held me in her embrace just as my grandmother used to, which only made me gasp as I began to cry louder and louder.

Unshed tears don't go away; they just accumulate...

"It's okay, my son," she said to me as my tears slowly began to subside. We stood there silently for a while until I finally lifted my head off her gentle shoulder. She then slowly stepped back and looked me in the eyes:

"What happened to you, my son?"

"I lost my way..."

"We all do," she replied gently.

"I'm so sorry..."

"You don't have to be anymore. You are forgiven."

"Is this a dream?"

"Life is a dream," she said.

"What happened to all the guards?"

"They are not needed anymore..."

HOME

MAMA

You're quieter than you used to be,
and you look like you haven't slept for seventeen years.
I'm here for you, mama…

You were wise,
not to buy me that Superman suit,
because I was planning to fly off our rooftop,
with the rest of those Arabian birds you disliked so much.
I'm here for you, mama…

Do you remember the first time our eyes met?
You probably didn't realize it,
but that was the first time you taught me,
how to see the dignity,
that God had placed like a precious pearl,
within the depth of every human soul.
I'm here for you, mama…

Does it matter that my tears,
are now flowing down my face,
and onto this page,
stirring these words to blossom,
into sad willow trees,
gently swaying in the wind?
I'm here for you, mama…

I'm sorry I didn't listen.
My wings were clipped,
and I was thrown down a bottomless well,
in which I kept descending,
for six thousand days,
and six thousand nights,
until the earth itself inverted,
and the many wills below,
bowed down to the only will above.
I'm here for you, mama…

WHERE IS MY FATHER?

I know...
I know that a few lines of poetry
won't fill the gap between us.

Missed years
and missed tears.
Regardless of the reasons,
I wasn't there
to bear
your pain.

You faced the world without a shield
insecurities concealed.
Where is my father?
Why bother?

Days passed on,
one after another,
piling on,
until the sun of hope was blocked,
Shocked!
by how cruel some people could be.
Maybe one day,
we'll see again,
eye
to
eye.

Regardless,
I'm here now,
waiting for you,
as you once waited,
for so long...

HOME

S hortly after my release, I was part of a virtual meeting led by two professors who invited former prisoners from the United States and Canada to discuss the concept of "home" from a philosophical perspective.

Some of those present had spent up to 33 years inside and had just recently been released. My 17 years felt like baby time in comparison. At one point, one of the professors asked us to write down three adjectives that described our post-prison experience. Most of the entries displayed on the screen began with adjectives like "exciting," "euphoric," and "magical" but ended with "lonely," "overwhelming," and "confidence shattering."

Anyone listening to the conversation would have quickly realized that these individuals had done a lot of work on themselves and were now completely transformed human beings. I guess this is precisely why it was so painful to witness how rejected and unseen many of them felt.

It is not difficult to understand why members of society would feel hesitant, afraid, and judgmental of someone who has committed a major crime in the past. And yet this makes it no less tragic for someone to endure the horrific prison system, redeem themselves despite it, and finally return home, only to realize that the locks are still there, just not physically.

∞

To finally make it home,
only to realize,
there is no home,
for (you).

You see it,
in the quick flicker of their eyes,
the body adjustment,
the change in tone,
the step back, even,
but that's okay,
because my home has never been of this world.
I am Aladdin,
and when I stand on my prayer mat,
time collapses,
into the illusion that it is;
and the distance between heaven and earth,
vanishes...

RIOT GEAR

I am extinguished now.
It's surrender all the way,
from this point on.

"STOP RESISTING!"
I remember the guards yelling at us,
in their riot gear,
on our first day inside.

Nearly two decades later,
I finally understand.

SEA OF CIRCUMSTANCES

As I ride the bus back home,
on a sunny afternoon,
amidst a sea of traffic,
I sense a higher order,
carrying us all,
upon a sea of circumstances,
beyond the shores of our own choosing.
And so, my heart is flooded
with a calming peace,
for I now know,
that all I must do,
is surrender...

Not Savages!

At the age of 16, Nolan Turcotte became yet another indigenous prison statistic. Today, he is 32 years old and still remains behind bars, serving an indefinite sentence. According to Statistics Canada, Indigenous adults represent only 4.1 percent of the overall Canadian population, and yet in 2016, they formed almost *30 percent* of total custodial admissions. I performed this poem for an audience at the Toronto Reference Library.

∞

Nolan,
Sitting here before dawn prayer,
Thinking of you,
Mentally reaching out to you.
Wherever you may be
I pray you'll be free
One day at a time
Sublime
Divine
These words are *not* mine.

Remember...
Remember when we first met?
No, it was no movie set,
I bet
you remember
December
in the lion's den
First days in the Pen
young cub
SHU club
now look at you!

You're closer than you think
Don't blink
Or sink
Just follow the traces of my ink
and we'll meet again
and again
Somewhere between these lines
are signs
for those who see
BREAK FREE!

Break free with your kindness,
with your manners,
with your words,
with your prayers,
with every *ounce* of goodness in you,
with everything *you got!*
Because We. All. Need. You!

Until then...
Remind them,
again and again,
THAT WE
ARE
NOT
SAVAGES!

THE MOUNTAINS SPEAK NOW

This is my first Ramadan fast beyond the gates of prison. Last night, I woke up before dawn to prepare for the day's fast, but something felt different, so I sat down and started writing.

∞

Soul unburdened
Sight unhindered
Lightness within me
Lifts me upwards.

Wings angelic
Bright stars shining
The path is straight now
I see it clearly.

Unforced smile bursts
Gentle teardrops
My soul is free now
The gates have opened.

Surrender, surrender
I hear the melody
The mountains speak now
and the trees are bowing!

INVICTUS

I am functionally delusional.
Each morning, I launch my fragile dreams heavenwards,
like a deck of cards,
certain they will land in perfect order.
While my mind points out my flawed logic,
my soul is spurred on by it,
like a black wild stallion crashing through the gates.
Invictus,
I cannot be defeated...

Nightmares and Daydreams II

A year ago, I was sitting in a prison cell, marking my seventeenth year inside, unsure if I could handle another rejection from the Parole Board.

Today, I'm sitting on a bus, on my way to work, unsure if this is just a daydream waiting to be shattered by a rude awakening.

It's surreal how the seemingly immovable mountains of circumstance can suddenly evaporate.

Most people wonder, *How does it feel?*

Magical, but equally unbelievable.

After six thousand and twenty-two mornings of waking up to the same depressing site of that stubborn steel door, to the clanking sound of keys, to the bright flashlights of guards checking on you for signs of life, not because they cared—although some genuinely did—but because they could lose their jobs if you died on their watch.

"Count 'em like diamonds and treat 'em like shit."

And lastly, to the heartbreaking sight of the methadone-*ians* who were beckoned from their slumber to their daily dose of government-sponsored synthetic heroin, which sucked the colour from their faces and gave them eyes one would expect to find in a Tolkien novel.

"Our demons do not haunt us at nighttime," I once read, "They strike in the morning. We are at our most vulnerable when we wake, for that is when the memory of who we are, and how we got here, returns."

Even better was Solzhenitsyn's observation: "The shock of wrongful arrest, followed by a ten- or twenty-year sentence, the baying of the guard dogs, the sound of escort troops priming their rifles, the nerve-racking jangle of morning call in the camps, seep through all the strata of ordinary experience, through all their secondary and even primary instincts, into a prisoner's very bones so that, sleeping, he remembers that he is in jail before he becomes aware of smoke or the smell of burning and gets up to find the place on fire."

So, how does it feel to wake up one morning outside this suffocating Matrix?

It's like preparing yourself to squat a thousand pounds, and just as you direct every ounce of force you have upwards—NOTHING!

Standing, almost jumping, nearly falling...

That's what it feels like—confusing, disorienting, enchanting, exhilarating, and uplifting—the five stages of sudden relief.

But that feeling doesn't last forever because life always moves on —a never-ceasing treadmill that's constantly moving you forward to the tragic and exhilarating experience of being alive.

So don't give up just because your life has suddenly turned into a nightmare.

Nightmares end,
and so do daydreams.
God, on the other hand,
is forever...

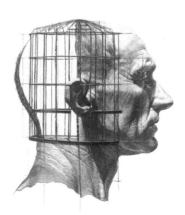

Recollections of a Returning Citizen

A year after my release, Professor Kim Maclaren asked me to write about my re-entry experience. This story was published by *The Philosopher*, the U.K's longest-running public philosophy journal.

∞

I am writing this under emotional duress.
Professor Kym Maclaren has invited me to write during a season which bears no fruitful words for me.

She is an angel.
I can't let her down.
So, here I am.

Why am I struggling to write this?

Prison...
A word of Latin origin, migrating to France before making England its home.

Prison...
My involuntary home for seventeen years.

Prison...
A place that teaches you how to say goodbye to friends.

Perhaps I should start there.

Saying goodbye to friends...

Change of rhythm.

Saying goodbye to friends was always bittersweet.

Sweet, because they were free again.

And bitter, because I was always the one who remained behind.

"Your turn will come," a friend once said to me, "the more people you see leave, the closer you are to the end of the line."

Words that served me well, until that fateful day finally arrived.

Professor Maclaren wants me to get into more detail here.

How did it feel?

Shocking, yet destined to be.

Most people don't understand just how difficult it is to be granted conditional release on a life sentence. The fact that I was —*and I realize this is coming from left field*— a convicted terrorist, made this outcome even more...

Even more...

Forgive me, but articulating the odds eludes me, so allow me instead to list everyone who needed to be persuaded:

> Parole Officers: Yes (Shannon and Robin were angels!)
> Their Supervisor: Yes
> Prison Security Department: Yes
> Psychology Department: Yes
> Community Residential Facility: Yes
> Local Police: Yes
> Canada's Anti-Terrorism Task Force (in an unprecedented two-day voluntary interrogation): Yes
> Parole Board of Canada: Yes

I suspect that even Richard Dawkins would secretly admit that divine intervention may have been necessary to convince all these risk-averse voices to arrive at the humanly seldom-reached island of unanimous consent.

That's a wordy sentence.

What happens next? The professor is prodding me on.

I'm pulling teeth here.

Two weeks of discomfort and anxious anticipation.

That was the period between the decision to grant me parole and my actual release. I don't have to explain the anxious anticipation, that you can understand. The discomfort, however, came from the fact that I was no longer a genuine member of the inmate population. I felt like an imposter, or perhaps I was just grappling with survivor's guilt.

It's hard to make eye contact with someone you're leaving behind
in hell.

A moment of silence...

Don't tell anyone, but some of us believed that capital punishment was more humane.

Now you know... why this is so hard to write.

Then...

Then the day arrived when I finally walked past the forbidden gates and felt an indescribable sensation of euphoric magic pulsing through every fiber of my being.

I feel awkward writing this, but there is no smooth way to transition from hell.

My sister was waiting for me in her car as I walked out *unescorted*.

A man who was paralyzed from the waist down suddenly begins to walk. His movements are shaky as he extends his arms outwards, hoping to regain an ancient balance he vaguely remembers but has not felt for 17 years...

I felt my brain slowly rewiring itself as it began shedding its barbed wire knots...
The arbitrators of summer's end had declared it over,
but it was still *here*,
saving its very best *for me*.

For most of my time inside, there was always an ugly grey mesh obscuring my sight from the heavens.

Not today.

I can go on describing this period forever, but I must move on to what inevitably follows every peak experience,

Disillusionment.

Disillusionment at the Mandela-esque realization that after every mountain climbed in life, there is always another peak to conquer.

I am tempted to end here, but I can hear Professor Maclaren urging me to say more, to unpack, to explain.

Starting over at the age of thirty-eight, with a criminal record and heavy restrictions on communication, association, and movement, was incredibly challenging. But hardest of all was my deep yearning to reconnect with the community that I once tried to harm.

*I wanted society to hug me,
but winter, here in the north, is cold.*

The halfway house I lived in was stuffed with granola bars. They were literally everywhere; at the reception desk, in the kitchen, in my drawers, and even under my bed.

I remember trying to approach total strangers on the street and offering them granola bars. Looking back, I realize just how *strange* my behaviour must have come across to these strangers.

> *I wanted society to hug me,*
> *but winter, here in the north, is cold.*

Then came the practical stuff.

Getting my lost identification felt like trying to assemble a jigsaw puzzle with half the pieces missing.

Finding a job. Who wants to hire someone with a criminal record, let alone a convicted terrorist?

> *Conclude on an upbeat note.*

But in life, there are always opportunities waiting just around the corner.

> *Professor Maclaren is asking me to expand on this.*
> *I am tired.*
> *Time to cheat.*

I've been out for fifteen months/I have a full-time job/I have an upcoming book titled *The Boy and his Sandcastle: A Journey of Redemption*/and I consult for ETAtoronto.ca, an organization that helps youth who have fallen prey to violent extremism.

I am exhausted now.

Goodbye.

∞

The Boy Returns

The world often conspires to make us doubt our inherent goodness, and perhaps there is no place where this truth is more keenly felt than in modern prisons.

There is nothing rehabilitative *here*.

Just the singular message, repeated over and over again, through a multitude of spoken and unspoken means, stating in no uncertain terms, *that you are inherently flawed... that you are inherently irredeemable.*

And so, after seventeen years of enduring this relentless message that reverberates within the echoing cinderblock walls and twists through the unbending steel bars, it is not difficult to understand how it can eventually extinguish the memory *that you were once good... that you were once innocent.*

Now, a year has passed since my release, and I have been granted permission to stay over at my brother's home.

I am in the basement, dawn is breaking, and the lights are off,

I've said my prayers, and I am filled with guilt.

Guilt for being me.

As I sit silently struggling to come to terms with who I am and how I got here, I look to my left and spot a brown notebook between a stack of old DVDs.

As I grab it, I notice the following words written on its cover in black marker:

"The Notebook and Memories of Zakaria."

Curiously, I begin to sift through its pages as I slowly yet instantly realize that I am reading a journal that I kept when I was just eleven years old, a year before emigrating to Canada.

"Reconnect with your inner child" was advice I often came across during my extensive prison readings. But as someone prone to skepticism, I was not convinced this was possible, given the tenuous nature of human memory and the inherent subjective bias in all our perceptions.

Here, however, was a document authored by *me* when I *was* a child.

Some things can't be explained with words alone...

"The Notebook and Memories of Zakaria
– Volume 1 – Under the supervision of Zakaria."

مذكرة ١٩٩٥
Luxe 1995

Fingerprints of my childhood friends.

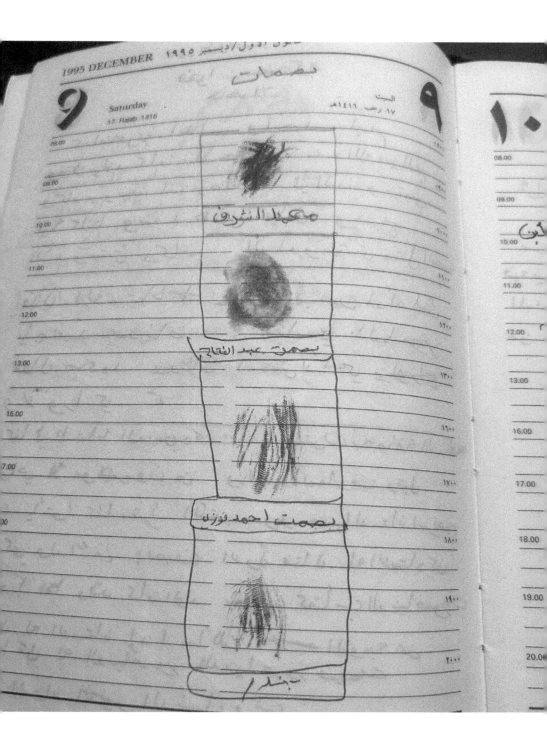

My favourite cartoons.

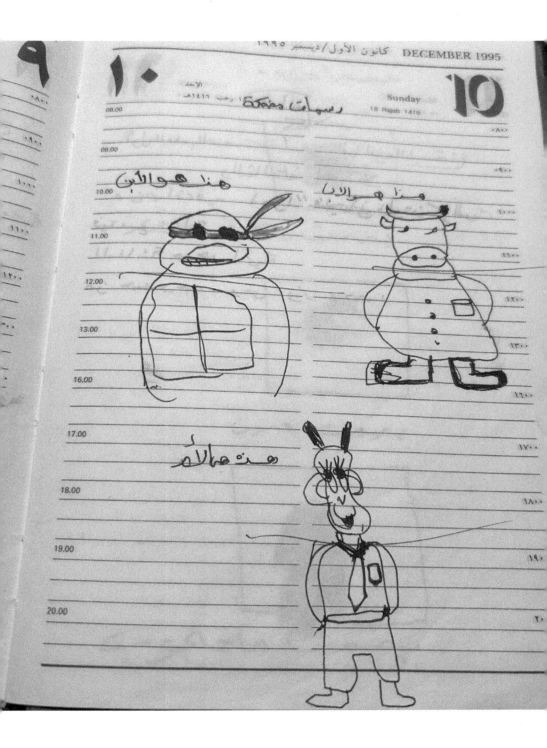

*"Gold Mine: The little man on the left says,
'I am digging for gold!'"*

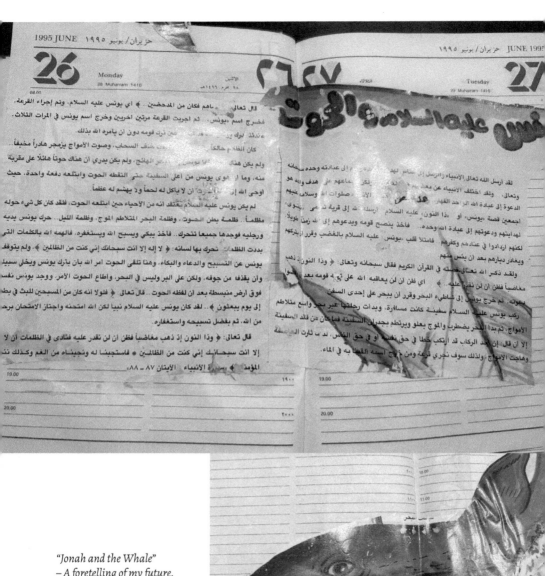

"Jonah and the Whale"
– A foretelling of my future.

But as I reached the end, the final entry left me shaken.

A gun with a message...

"No to death.
No to killing.
No to evil."

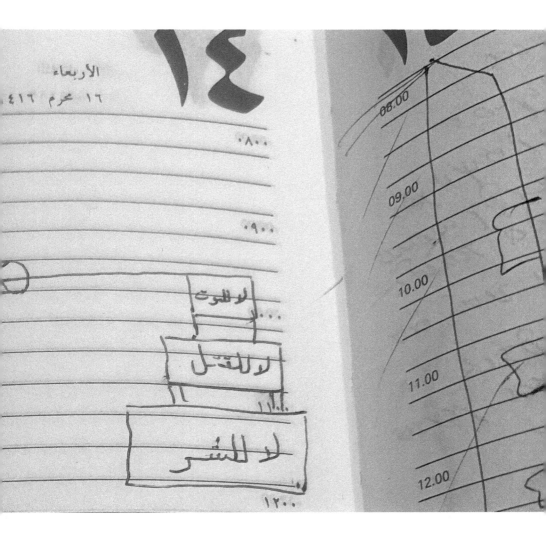

Suddenly, decades of distorted messaging that stood like concrete barriers between the man I am and the child I was came crashing down.

I could see him now. *Feel him*, close, warm, still breathing. And somehow still alive.

A boy emerging from beneath the rubble, *heart first*.

He has returned.

About the designer (and the project)

My name is Agata Filipczak, though my friends call me Nio. I live in Poland (Central Europe) and am a designer with a "classical education." I graduated from the Academy of Fine Arts in Lodz with a Master of Arts degree.

For many years, I worked for an international press corporation, reaching the top position of Art Director for the Polish branch. After several years, I resigned due to becoming more immersed in office politics and less involved in actual design work. My partner, also a designer and the love of my life, resigned from his corporate career as well. That's when we created Niokoba, the creative studio we launched 12 years ago to focus on what we love - design.

Niokoba is an invented word that doesn't exist in any language. It was formed using the first syllables of Polish words meaning "not mincing matters." We design book covers, publications, and magazines. Our clients seem to think we're rather good at it!

From my corporate years, I kept the efficient workflow mechanisms implemented in my studio. I also maintained my interest in politics. I believe avoiding difficult subjects fails to improve anything. On the contrary, whether you follow politics or not, it takes a keen interest in you.

The Boy and His Sandcastle

Zak contacted me through Fiverr, like many clients before and after him. But his words held a special emotional weight - I instantly knew this wouldn't be just another project.

We corresponded as Zak polished the manuscript, exchanging ideas and observations on the project. Despite the thousands of miles between us, we seemed to think alike.

When the final draft was ready, we spoke with Zak. We finalized details and established a working relationship. Most importantly, I felt honored by the tremendous gift of trust Zak had granted me - he placed his dream and greatest treasure into my hands.

Now, as we near completion, I can say this has become one of the most meaningful projects in my career. I'm incredibly grateful to Zak for the creative freedom and confidence he has given me. I'm also glad he decided to publish this book rather than hide it away unpublished. It's a story everyone should read.

Design Process Notes

I read the memoir manuscript. This book is impressive and mesmerizing.

Key associations for the project:

- Journey through time and space
- Transformation (convey subtly)
- Mistakes and suffering are universal
- A world needing repair - it cries out for kintsugi
- Can one truly live while dying inside?

Dream sequences vs. reality: In dreams, Zak finds freedom outside of prison (his spirit breaks free). Convey through simple, unembellished layouts and pure, austere compositions.

Chapter illustrations evolve gradually from despair toward light and life.

Cover Concepts

- A single drop can drill even the hardest basalt rock over time.
- Brightness lives inside Zak - he has left the darkness behind him. Avoid the shadow - the shadow never leaves you, and Zak has closed that door.
- Sand = tiny pieces of rock ;-)
- Castle = ghostly mansion, demons of the past
- The moon - the only companion in despair
- Light/dark, not black/white!

ACKNOWLEDGEMENTS

Mama
Mama
Mama
Baba
Ramzi
Dena
Sitto
Seedo
Yaya
Papoo
Christakis
Samar
Fatima
Huda
Ahmad
Juma
Dawood
Nabeel
Mahmood
Nada D
Nada
Nour
Mama Farida
Baba Farooq
Sidra
Hana
Raza
Rana
Hamza
Reem
Umm Ahmed
Ali
Abdulbari
Nikos
Dimitris
Abdullah
Ameer
Omar
MAV
Umair
Saad
Ibrahim
Jamal
Zahra
Sukaina
Umm Sukaina
Reem
Charyfa
Nadia
Mikaeel
Juliane
Gary
Art
Sharm
Sheryl
Sashanny
Nour
Catherine
Jacob
Brandan
Dena W
Jovan
Jim
John
Vaishali
Kassandra
Jessica
Shaqilla
Ansel

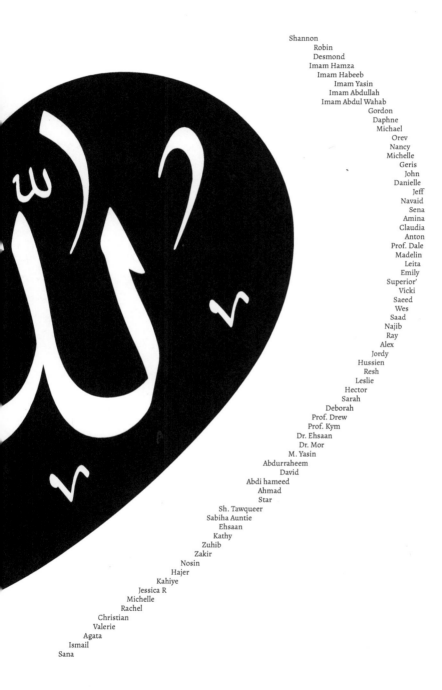

Shannon
Robin
Desmond
Imam Hamza
Imam Habeeb
Imam Yasin
Imam Abdullah
Imam Abdul Wahab
Gordon
Daphne
Michael
Orev
Nancy
Michelle
Geris
John
Danielle
Jeff
Navaid
Sena
Amina
Claudia
Anton
Prof. Dale
Madelin
Leita
Emily
Superior'
Vicki
Saeed
Wes
Saad
Najib
Ray
Alex
Jordy
Hussien
Resh
Leslie
Hector
Sarah
Deborah
Prof. Drew
Prof. Kym
Dr. Ehsaan
Dr. Mor
M. Yasin
Abdurraheem
David
Abdi hameed
Ahmad
Star
Sh. Tawqueer
Sabiha Auntie
Ehsaan
Kathy
Zuhib
Zakir
Nosin
Hajer
Kahiye
Jessica R
Michelle
Rachel
Christian
Valerie
Agata
Ismail
Sana

Milton Keynes UK
Ingram Content Group UK Ltd.
UKHW052257280324
439855UK00009B/17